ALEXANDER POPE

A CRITICAL STUDY OF HIS MAJOR POEMS

M.P. Sinha

ATLANTIC

PUBLISHERS & DISTRIBUTORS (P) LTD

Published by
ATLANTIC
PUBLISHERS & DISTRIBUTORS (P) LTD

7/22, Ansari Road, Darya Ganj,
New Delhi-110002
Phones : +91-11-40775252, 23273880, 23275880, 23280451
Fax : +91-11-23285873
Web : www.atlanticbooks.com
E-mail : orders@atlanticbooks.com

Branch Office
5, Nallathambi Street, Wallajah Road,
Chennai-600002
Phones : +91-44-64611085, 32413319
E-mail : chennai@atlanticbooks.com

ISBN 978-81-269-1559-0

Printed in India at Nice Printing Press, A-33/3A, Site-IV, Industrial Area, Sahibabad, Ghaziabad, U.P.

Preface

The aim of this book is to provide a critical analysis of Alexander Pope's major poems like *The Eclogues*, *Windsor Forest*, *Essay on Criticism*, *An Essay on Man*, *The Rape of the Lock*, *An Epistle to Dr Arbuthnot* and *The Dunciad*. The eighteenth century was basically the age of reason which looked down upon sentimentalism and romanticism as aberrations from the normal, natural and well-cultured life. All creative writers assumed the role of social reformers. They advised people to follow "plain living and high thinking".

Pope was a satirist, no doubt, but his attitude to life was not negative. Behind all his writings, there is a coherent philosophy of life. With the advent of the renaissance and rise of humanism, the old ideas of the medieval period were seriously challenged in the second half of the sixteenth century and the first half of the seventeenth century. A compromise was made in the eighteenth century, and the relationship between God, nature and man was defined in a new way. Pope's *Essay on Criticism* and *An Essay on Man* describe the relationship between God, nature, man, art and society. *Windsor Forest*, *The Rape of the Lock*, *An Epistle to Dr Arbuthnot* and *The Dunciad* are structured on Pope's philosophy of life and his poetic theory.

Poetry is an integral part of syllabus of English Hons. and postgraduation in English in all Indian universities. But it has been observed that the students do not read the prescribed poems, simply because they find them difficult and are unable to comprehend the hidden meaning or underlying idea and the effectiveness of poetic devices like similes, metaphors, alliteration etc. used by the poet. *Alexander Pope: A Critical Study of His Major Poems* has been written in simple language and lucid style to enable the students understand and appreciate Pope better. Apart from taking up the major poems of this celebrated poet, an exclusive chapter has been devoted to his style and technique.

The book will prove useful to the students and teachers of English literature, English poetry, particularly of Alexander Pope and researchers in these fields.

I am thankful to Dr K.R. Gupta, Honorary Advisor, Atlantic Publishers and Distributors (P) Ltd and Mr Harjeet Singh Publishing Co-ordinator, for publishing this book in a short time.

M.P. Sinha

Contents

1

Pope and His Age

Pope belongs to the eighteenth century which is popularly known as the Neo-classical or Augustan Age. The main reason for calling the eighteenth century Neo-classical or Augustan Age is that the poets of this period were highly inspired by Aristotle, Horace, Longinus, Homer, Virgil, Ovid, Bion, Theocritus and Dante. Although the Elizabethan poets were highly influenced by the classical Greek and Roman writers, yet they did not follow the poetic theory rigidly. On the other hand, Dryden, Pope Addison and Dr. Johnson almost replicated the classical writers.

The question is: Why did the late seventeenth century and the eighteenth century writers choose the classical Greek and Roman conventions as their model? The answer is that they found a close similarity between their own age and the classical Greek and Roman ages.

The preceding age, that is, the seventeenth century was a period of turmoil and conflict. The reign of James I was the period of religious conflict and it was soon followed by the violent period of Charles I and the reign of Cromwell. Things began to settle after the return of Charles II. But, after his death, the successor, James II, a catholic, could not maintain the equilibrium the country needed. The Glorious Revolution of 1688 settled the matter and from that time onwards England enjoyed calmness and certified till the First World War in the twentieth century.

If we look at the English history, we find that it is checkered with the wars between the royal families for the throne. The

Wars of the Roses that lasted for a long time involved all the nobility of England and led to the decline of the aristocracy. Besides, the developments in the tools of production made the middle class prosperous. By the end of the sixteenth century, the middle class comprising carpenters, shoemakers, blacksmiths, goldsmiths, weavers and other professionals groups became as rich as the old aristocracy. This rise in wealth led the middle class compete with the aristocracy in all walks of life. The first was political equality. The Parliament of England was divided into the House of Lords and the House of Commons. In the beginning, the lower house was not strong but by the beginning of the eighteenth century, it became equal in status and power. Literature could not escape the influence of the middle class. The rise of the citizen drama is an evidence of the fact that the creative writers shifted their attention from kings and dukes to the middle class and, in course of time, the rise of the novel made it amply clear that the middle class had became equal in social status in relation to the aristocracy.

The balance between the aristocracy and the middle class led to an equilibrium in the English society. This equilibrium is most evidently perceptible in the literature of the eighteenth century. David Daiches rightly says:

> It must be remembered that there was a correlation between social class and education, between elegance and learning, that has not always existed in subsequent periods....

In fact, the decline of aristocracy was first reflected in the Restoration Comedy where the lecherous and decadent life of the nobility was badly exposed. Congreve, Vanbrugh, Farquahar and Sheridan exposed the bawdy life of the aristocracy. The writers of the eighteenth century strove to chasten morality by means of satire. There are two ways to instruct people. The first is to preach in high sounding, lofty and abstract words and the second is to laugh mildly at abnormality, idiosyncrasy and aberration from the moral path. The eighteenth century writers chose the second method to lead people to the path of virtue and high morality. They rejected the aristocratic way of life and pleaded for the establishment of the time-hallowed middle class morality.

The second reason for accepting the middle class morality was that this class was in ascendancy and most of the writers came from this class. It was quite easy for them to speak of the ideas of the landed gentry and the manufacturers. Bonamy Dobreé in the *Early Eighteenth Century Literature* volume of *Oxford History of English Literature* writes:

> In the seventeenth century literature in main sprang from and was addressed to a society living by the idea of semi-divine royalist authority, with its most fruitful contentions and its deepest poetry concerned with religion. By 1750 literature belongs to a trading manufacturing society governed by an oligarchy, its dominating literature being concerned with morals—not Milton or Crashaw but Richardson and Dr. Johnson. What the upsurging middle class wanted in the early years of the century was to a large extent materially didactic literature; towards the middle it demanded the morally didactic.

However, it will be rash to say that everything was dominated by the middle class ethos. The fact is that many members of the aristocracy shifted to manufacture and trade. They became members of the middle class by profession but retained their own sense of morality and social norms. Secondly, the aristocracy still dominated the political scene. So the rising middle class made a compromise with the aristocracy. David Daiches very rightly says in *A Critical History of English Literature*:

> The Glorious Revolution of 1688, when James II was replaced by William of Orange and his wife Mary in a movement largely engineered by the middle class, Protestant heart of England represented a victory of the town over the court. But if the town had defeated the court and had rejected the court's standards in manners and morals, it had now to find its own standards, to root itself in a social and ethical code. It needed educating in the trivialities of life, which hitherto had been the property of the court.... The town had defeated the court, and now the town had to be educated upto its new position. The education and the entertainment (where possible both together) of the middle classes now became a legitimate objective of literature.

The new ethos began with the publication of the periodicals edited by Daniel Defoe, Richard Steele and Joseph Addison in the beginning of the century and by Oliver Goldsmith and Dr. Johnson later. Steele's *The Tatler* and Addison's *The Spectator* built the edifice of the eighteenth century social and moral code. But it was Pope who assimilated the leading philosophical, religious and scientific ideas in his poetry and showed the middle class how they could apply the principle of the "golden mean" of Aristotle. He advised his countrymen to follow nature which is God's art. Before we go to read his concept of nature, art and poetry, it will be pertinent to know the eighteenth century concept of God, nature and art.

II

People in general mean by nature, flora and fauna, rivers and mountains, lakes, seas and valleys. Even the stars and planets are supposed to be a part of nature. *Concise Oxford English Dictionary* defines nature as "the phenomena of the physical world collectively, including plants, animals, and the landscape, as opposed to humans or human creations".[1]

There is a difference between the common view of nature and the scientific view of nature. A scientist or philosopher understands nature as a system which operates behind all the growth and events of the world. For the common people, the outward appearance such as plants, trees, rivers, lakes, mountains, wild beasts and the objects not produced by human beings, is nature.

The poets of the sixteenth and seventeenth centuries took nature in the popular way. They were concerned with the beauty of nature. The sonnets of Wyatt and Surrey, the poems of Spenser, Sidney, Marlowe and Shakespeare are all about nature. Their love poems abound in natural imagery. The nineteenth century poets, too, praised the beauty of nature. Wordsworth, Coleridge, Shelley, Byron and Keats wrote poems on nature and its beauty. They did not take nature the way scientists and philosophers did. They were concerned with the outward manifestation of nature. Of course, Wordsworth considered nature a spirit, the spirit that leads man to perfection, but he ignored the scientific point of view.

The eighteenth century writers accepted the scientific explanation of nature. Till the blossoming of the renaissance the popular view of nature dominated. With the coming of Copernicus and Galileo, a section of scientists and philosophers began to make distinction between nature and its manifestations. The focus shifted to the laws of nature. Although the University wits were influenced by the humanism of the renaissance, they did not pay proper attention to the system of nature. The metaphysicals accepted the new challenges of philosophy and science but for them nature existed in the form of landscape and the animal world. Even Milton, who was aware of the new system of the universe, followed the old idea of the Great Chain of Being in *Paradise Lost*.

It was only towards the end of the seventeenth century that creative writers began to accept the scientific concept of nature. For writers like Dryden, Addison, Swift, Pope, Dr. Arbuthnot, Dr. Johnson, and Goldsmith, nature was a system and part of God's vast design. The contributions of Bacon and Newton were of cardinal importance.

The previous model of the universe was that there was heaven at the top and below it were different spheres of archangels, angels and lesser spirits. The earth was in the middle of the universe and the heavenly bodies like the sun, the moon and the stars revolved round the earth. At the bottom was hell, dark and deep, as described in Milton's *Paradise Lost*. People believed that the earth was formed from the chaos. The earth as a centre was surrounded by water and then by air. By "water" they meant all kinds of fluids. The watery surface of the globe had a top coating of oil. Further, before the process of creation had quite settled down, the air was full of dust. All this shifted down and formed a thick crust by mixing with the oily matter on the surface and became the first crust of the present-day world.

Copernicus rejected the old idea of the universe. He proved that the earth is not the centre of the universe and the sun does not move round it. On the contrary, it is the earth that moves round the sun. His discovery of the scientific truth antagonised the Church and he had to sacrifice his life while defending his new discovery. Galileo was imprisoned for saying that there are spots in the sun. His telescope was called the Devil's Eye. However, his followers carried the torch of the new knowledge and by the end of the seventeenth century the whole of Europe began to follow new science. In India, Aryabhatta of Pataliputra, told the people in the fifth century that the earth moves round the sun but unfortunately, he did not find courageous disciples who would hand down the new knowledge to the next generation. People's apathy blocked the progress of science in India. The greatest enemies of Aryabhatta were the orthodox Sanatanis.

The developments in science and philosophy made a great impact on art and literature of the eighteenth century. The place of God was not challenged. He remained the Supreme Being and Creator of the universe. The sun became the centre of the solar system and the earth its planet. Nature remained the same but the focus was not on the objects but on the system. It became the operative system of God's vast design. Martin C. Battestin writes:

> Science played an important part in producing the divinised 'nature' of the eighteenth century. The scientific discoveries and inventions of Copernicus, Kepler and Galileo produced a climate of opinion in which supernatural and occult explanations ceased to satisfy the scientist and the universe came more and more to be regarded as a Great Machine working by rigidly determined laws of material causation. This view involved a changed attitude towards nature; that nature was rescued from Satan and restored to God.[2]

The eighteenth century named "the silver age of the European renaissance" virtually began in the final decades of the seventeenth century. It was the golden age of natural theology. Newton's law of gravitation was adopted in theology, art and poetry. In nature, the principle of attractions and laws of inertia ruled supreme. If the planets and stars did not fall or collide, the reason was the principle of attractions and the laws of inertia. They remained positioned and in perfect balance.

The age of Pope is called the age of reason. Reason controls our desires, emotions and thoughts and tries to maintain a balance between conflicting ideas and emotions. Perhaps the best assessment of the period has been made by Legouis and Cazamian in their monumental *History of English Literature*. They write:

> One may say that the age of Pope lives more fully, more spontaneously at the pitch of that dominant intellectuality, which during the preceding age was chiefly an irresistible impulse, a kind of contagious intoxication. The Restoration had turned Reason herself into a free, adventurous guide; classicism now makes her a clear and calm adviser. Set modes of thought have now been formed, habits acquired and fixed.[3]

The eighteenth century writers, whether theologians or aesthetes, assumed the role of adviser and appealed to the people to follow reason and have absolute faith in God and His justice. Any kind of aberration, eccentricity or even deviation from the norm was unpardonable. They all advised people to follow nature and be natural.

The concept of nature was quite different from that of the previous century. Earlier, say in ancient times and even in the middle ages, nature was something mysterious and disorderly. People praised the beauty of nature in daytime but at night it was dark and sinister. The eighteenth century people developed a new model of the universe. God was the creator and nature was His art. Since they all believed in God's justice, they considered Him the "Supreme Reason". There was order, symmetry and harmony in God's design, they argued. Nature, as such, had these features. We will elaborate these features one by one.

Order

There is an order in the universe of things. The solar system works in perfect order. All the planets move round the sun with uniform speed. There is no aberration. If there is any deviation in the movement, there will not be regularity in the occurrence of day and night and the change of seasons. All planets and stars have their regular path.

Symmetry

Order leads to symmetry. The seventeenth century idea of "there is order in disorder" or "method in madness" is rejected. Things must be properly arranged. Things lying in disorder may appear to be organized in order but, after all, they are disorderly. For symmetry, there is the need that they are organized neatly and logically. In nature, everything is in symmetry. Each variety of plant and each species of the animal kingdom has its proportionate size and features.

Harmony

There is harmony in nature. Each object is complementary to the other. There is variety. Various things are not always in consonance. There are oppositions and contrasts. We can ask with Blake the question "Did He make the lamb/ Who made thee?" If there is the meek lamb, there is the ferocious tiger; if there is the rabbit, there is the python. The principle of harmony resolves all the contrasting and conflicting elements into a composite whole. Hopkins accepted this concept of nature in his famous curtal sonnet "Pied Beauty".

> All things counter, original, spare, strange;
> Whatever is fickle, freckled (who knows how?)
> With swift, slow, sweet, sour; adazzle, dim;
> He fathers forth whose beauty is past change; Praise him.[4]

The eighteenth century poets laid emphasis on the relationship between nature and art. Nature is created by God and art by man. As in all walks of our life we follow God's light, we should follow Him in art also. Since nature is God's art, man's art should initiate nature, that is, it should have order, symmetry and harmony besides regularity. M. Battestin has admirably summarised the eighteenth century concept of the relation between nature and art:

> From the Rennaissance, the Neo-classical poets inherited two levels of nature: Imperfect and Perfect. Perfect nature is the orderly system of harmony, and ideal beauty, which

> God called into being, at the beginning of the time. It is the perfect nature that art improves upon reality.
>
> The Augustans regarded the ideal nature as a kind of redeemer, offering them bright images of Paradise and turning their thoughts to the music of creation. They considered God as a Supreme Creator whose art is, of course, nature. It means God or Divine creates nature and man only imitates and reflects that creation. There was a firm belief that 'Art' is the imitation of Nature; the imperfect human art imitates the perfect art of nature, which is really, the divine art itself. So the formal characteristics of nature—harmony, symmetry and proportion—would also be the characteristic of art.[5]

III

Alexander Pope (1688-1744) is the dominant poetic figure of the Augustan period. In fact, he is the greatest of the literary figures who wrote best on the relationship between nature and art. When he advised people to follow nature he did not mean "nature" as it was understood by the seventeenth century poets or by Wordsworth towards the end of the eighteenth century. To Wordsworth, nature stood for the eternal force, the shaping spirit, that leads man to perfection and saves him from the corrupting gross materialism of the industrial society. For him, there was a sharp contrast between the town and the country. If the town was a corrupting place the country, ensconced in the lap of nature, was an invigorating place. Pope looked at nature as art of God, rational, orderly, symmetrical and harmonious. He described nature as, at once, the source, end and test of art.

Art, Pope declared, must follow God's art, that is, nature. It is a fact that "nature" of one age becomes the "art" of the next and each school has to fight against the "nature" of the last age. Both art and nature require the adherence of reason and good sense. So the solution is to identify nature and follow the ancient tradition of Homer and Virgil, their rules and sound reason.

Pope's concept of nature and art is based on following three main principles:

(a) All sound judgement and true wit are founded on the observation of nature.

(b) False wit arises from the disregard of nature.

(c) The true standard for determining what is natural in poetry is to be found in the best works of the ancients.

His first principle is expressed in these lines of *Essay on Criticism*:

First follow Nature, and your judgement frame
By her just standard, which is still the same.

A true wit or poet must observe how nature functions. In nature, everything is regular and systematic, symmetrical and harmonious. Likewise poetry and art should be proportionate (in the Aristotelian sense), symmetrical and harmonious. This is why the preferred metre is iambic pentameter with a caesura in the middle to balance the preceding and following feet. The lines must rhyme to be in balance and harmony. So the most popular stanza form is the heroic couplet. By the use of the heroic couplet the progress of a poem is made slow and majestic.

He, like the Augustans, says that nature is God's art. He writes in *Essay on Man*.

All Nature is but Art, unknown to thee;
All chance, Direction, which thou canst see.

He advises the young poets and artists to observe it minutely. If they pay attention to nature seriously, the things that appear to happen by chance are not disorderly. They have a direction; they are part of nature which is God's creation.

The great problem before the Augustans was to make distinction between nature and art. It was quite obvious that nature was God's art. Man was to follow it. Any deviation from nature was a kind of breaking away with God's wishes. The objects of nature maintained regularity, orderliness and harmony. Man too was to observe decorum, proportion and harmony in his personal and social life as well. In the seventeenth century, Ben Jonson followed the principle of humour that excess of any kind of humour would lead man to some kind of disease, physical or mental. With the development of science, the eighteenth century intellectuals rejected the concept of humour and turned to nature. Pope and his contemporaries wanted people to be natural, not artificial. They laid stress on simplicity and austerity and the control of reason on emotion.

The aim of art, then was to make people "natural", that is, to enable them to get rid of all kinds of pomp and show and the different subtle forms of the deadly sins.

While making the distinction between nature and art, Pope took the example of forest and garden. A forest is nature's creation. It is not livable for man. A garden is on the other hand, man's creation hence a work of art. The garden is still nature, but nature methodised. Pope constructed his own house and named it Twickenham Garden. The picture of his grand house gives us a good idea of the garden which is in imitation of the forest. Art to him is nature methodized:

> Those Rules of old discovered, not devised
> Are Nature still but nature methodised.

By old rules, he means the rules of nature. Nature has created all the objects of the world, man included. What a poet has to do is to discover them and follow them in a new way. The new rules he will use are his own method. These rules are founded on good sense and sound reason. According to Pope the ancients followed these rules in the highest degree and it is the duty of the moderns to know and adapt those rules of following nature. He writes:

> You then whose judgement the right course would steer,
> Know well each Ancient's proper character.

Finally, to Pope, nature is to be followed because it is revealed to us through our sense perception. Nature and art are inter-related. Although art imitates nature, yet it is not a blind imitation; it is nature still but nature methodized. It is the sophisticated form of nature in which the poet, equipped with the rules discovered by the great masters of the past, creates a new work. He takes utmost care that his work is not a distortion of nature. He knows the truth that nature is at once the source, end, and the test of art. In *Essay on Criticism*, stating that art should methodize nature, he exhorts the younger poets and his contemporaries:

> Learn hence for ancient rules a just esteem
> To copy nature is to copy them.

Here he means to say that the ancient writers like Homer, Aeschylus, Sophocles, Virgil and Dante were poets who followed nature truly. So if poets copy them, they also copy nature. Agreeing with the poet-critic Horace, he says that the real motives of poetry are rationality and good sense. Pope thus is a neo-classicist or Augustan in the true sense of the term. He best represents the intellectual background of his age. His greatness lies in universality. His ideas expressed in *An Essay on Man* are still true, even in the twenty-first century. We still follow the four broad divisions made by him: man in the universe, man in society, man to himself and man and happiness. Pope's poetry illustrates his poetic theory. His greatness lies in the fusion of his philosophy of life, poetic theory, profundity of thought and sparkling wit. Perhaps, he is the most quoted poet after Shakespeare.

Notes

1. *Concise Oxford English Dictionary* (1998), p. 950.
2. Martin C. Battestin, *The Providence of Wit: Aspects of Form in Augustan Literature and the Arts* (London: OUP, 1974), p. 22.
3. E. Legouis and L. Cazamian, *History of English Literature* (Delhi: Macmillan, 1997), p. 712.
4. H. Mekenzie, ed. *The Poems of Gerard Manley Hopkins* (London: OUP, 1960), p. 50.
5. Martin C. Battestin, *op. cit.*, p. 25.

2

The Eclogues and Windsor Forest

Alexander Pope was a precocious child. Even at the age of ten, he talked like an adult and his knowledge of literature was far advanced of his years. He began writing poetry at an early age. "Ode on Solitude", a poem he wrote at the age of twelve, is one of the most anthologised poems and we are struck with the calm serenity and fine craftsmanship of the poet.

> Happy the man, whose wish and care
> A few paternal acres bound,
> Content to breathe his native air
> In his own ground.

At that age Pope was fully immersed in the Elizabethan tradition of poetry and Edmund Spenser, poet's poet, was his model. One thing remarkable in this poem is that, in spite of his deformity and weak health, Pope had peace of mind. Besides harmony, which is one of the most important features of his poetry, he aspired for peace in his earliest poetry. It will be pertinent to quote G. Wilson Knight in this respect.

> At the start of the eighteenth century a new way of life was being established in England. The fruits of the Revolution were maturing. Under Queen Anne party politics were getting, if at first rather unsteadily, into their stride, as a safeguard against bloodier methods; new classes were rising rapidly to education, power and prestige; there was peace and renewal after distraction and unrest. The age of Anne recaptured, in its own fashion, something of that

> assurance, and more than something of the harmony, of the age of Elizabeth I. Its poet was Pope: "Be mine the blessings of a peaceful reign."
>
> Dante, Shakespeare and Pope all reflect a unified and harmonious life-view.[1]

Pope's poetic career began with the unified and harmonious life view at the young age of twelve in "Ode on Solitude" and four years later blossomed in the *Pastorals*, also called *Eclogues*, and reached fruition in the later poems. The beginning was in nature and maturity in the fusion of nature and art.

The *Pastorals* are nature poems written in the classical tradition. A pastoral poem is about the life of a shepherd who lives in the company of nature. Pope himself has given his views on pastoral poetry in his famous *Discourse*. It is surprising that at the age of sixteen he could write such an essay. Besides, his prose is very slightly different from that of the twentieth century.

> A pastoral is an imitation of the action of a shepherd, or one considered under that character. The form of this imitation is dramatic, or narrative, or mixed of both; the fable simple; the manners not too polite nor too rustic: the thoughts are plain, yet admit a little quickness and passion but that short and flowing : the expression humble yet as pure as the language will afford; neat but not florid; easy and yet lively. In short, the fable, manners, thoughts, and expressions are full of the greatest simplicity.[2]

As said earlier, the *Pastorals* are eclogues. An eclogue is a poem that describes the beauty of the seasons in a year and the narrator is, of course, a shepherd. The tradition of the eclogue is quite old. The Greek and Italian poets wrote eclogues. In India, Kalidasa's *Ritusambaram* is an eclogue. *Barahmasa*, a series of poems narrating the beauty of the twelve months of the year, is highly popular among the village people.

Pope writes about his pastorals or eclogues:

> The complete character of this poem consists in simplicity, brevity, and delicacy; the two first of which render an eclogue natural and the last delightful.[3]

The poem is divided into four sections. Each section is named after a season. The first section is named "Spring". Technically speaking, each section is a *verse count*. "Spring" is the longest *verse count* consisting of 102 lines. The first ten lines are a compliment to Sir William Trumbull. Sir William Trumbull was in his fifties, when Pope met him for the first time. Pope was at that time, less than ten. At the time of the poem's publication Pope was sixteen and Sir William above sixty. Sir William Trumbull was an important personality, highly educated and well-mannered. He had been ambassador to different countries and was finally a lord of the treasury.[4]

The first six lines are written, under the influence of Elizabethan and Italian poets, though they follow the eighteenth century convention, the heroic couplet.

> First in these fields I try the sylvan strains
> Nor blush to sport on Windsor's blissful plains
> Fair Thames, flow gently from thy sacred spring,
> While on thy banks Sicilian muses sing;
> Let vernal airs through trembling osiers play
> And Albion's Cliffs resound the rural lay.

[Eclogue I : Spring, lines 1-6]

This is the general exordium and opening of the pastorals in imitation of the sixth pastorals of Virgil. "In the beginnings of the other three pastorals, he imitates expressly those which now stand first of the three chief poets in this kind, Spenser, Virgil, Theocritus."[5]

The first line is significant. The three words—"fields", "Sylvan" and "strains"—indicate that the poem we are going to read is about nature. The phrase "Sylvan strains" is a bold experiment in word collocation. "Sylvan" generally means "of woods". It is only after Pope's use of the phrase that "Sylvan" has assumed the meaning "pastoral". The phrase "Windsor's plains" leads us to Sir William Trumbull who was born in Windsor-forest. The third line is evidently written in imitation of Spenser's lines of *Prothalamion*.

"Sweet Thames run softly till I end my song", which later on, T.S. Eliot quoted in *The Waste Land* in a different context.

Then Pope uses the phrase "Sicilian muses". Let us remember that Theocritus, father of pastoral poetry, was born in Sicily. Finally, Pope returns again to Windsor in the sixth line; the "Albion Cliffs" are the hills near Windsor.

The opening of the first section, "Spring", is very much rooted in nature. The words "fields", "sylvan", "strains", "plains", "Thames" and "Sicily" all are related to nature. The song of the spring season is produced by the passing of breeze through the osiers. We find that everything is full of joy, freshness and vivacity.

It is also to be seen that even at a young age of sixteen, Pope is well-versed in classical literature. He has read Virgil, Theocritus and Dante. Besides these, he has read the Elizabethan and the seventeenth century poets quite well. Here, of course, he is more influenced by Edmund Spenser.

The next six lines are the concluding part of the invocation. The invocation is in the true tradition of the past pastoral poetry.

> O let my muse her slender reed inspire,
> Till in your native shades you tune the lyre:
> So when the nightingale to rest removes,
> The thrush may chant to the forsaken groves
> But charmed to silence, listens while she sings,
> And all the aerial audience clap their wings.
>
> [Eclogue I]

The slender reed means the pipe a poet uses while singing. It is related to poetry also. In this invocation, the poet requests the goddess of poetry (Muse) to inspire him to sing of the spring season its morning when the night bird nightingale retires and the morning bird, the thrush starts singing. These lines we see, give us a beautiful depiction of nature in the morning. The audial imagery is worth appreciating—the reed, the lyre, the nightingale's song, the singing thrush and the clapping wings of birds. After the invocation the poet leads us to the Sylvan scene. We see the two Shepherds, Daphnis and Strephon, come to the scene at the sunrise.

Soon as the flocks shook off the nightly dews
Two swains, whom love kept wakeful, and the muse
Poured o'er the whitening vale their fleecy care,
Fresh as the morn, and as the season fair:
The dawn now blushing on the mountain's side,
Thus Daphnis spoke, and Strephon thus replied.

[Eclogue I]

If we ignore the iambic metre and the stanza pattern, this passage is as romantic as any one of Spenser or Keats. We should also bear in mind the fact that the classical poets like Theocritus and Horace used the heroic couplet in love poems and, so, the eighteenth century poets followed their path.

The other quality of an eclogue is that it is usually a dialogue between swains, shepherds or goatherds. Here "Spring" is a dialogue between Daphnis and Strephon. It is only at the end of the section that the third character, Damon, appears and gives the concluding speech. Daphnis is the first singer. He praises the morning's beauty:

Hear how the birds, on every bloomy spray,
With joyous music wake the dawning day!
Why sit we mute, when early linnets sing,
When warbling Philomel salutes the spring?
Why sit we sad, when Phosphor shines so clear,
And lavish nature paints the purple year?

[Eclogue I]

Since winter has passed and spring season is coming, the shepherds find the whole earth happy and joyful. The day is personified. The morning birds wake him with their joyful songs. The sweet singing nightingale welcomes the coming of the spring and the morning star Phosphor or Venus shines brightly in the sky. The generous nature has painted the coming year with bright colours. Pope's use of audial and visual imagery is praiseworthy. The images of the singing birds, the linnet and the nightingale are part of the audial imagery and the shining Venus and nature's paints (meaning flowers of various colours) are part of visual imagery. Daphnis says if the world of nature is so vivacious and mirthful they should not remain calm or sad and must sing the songs of the season's beauty.

> Sing then, and Damon shall attend the strain
> While you slow oxen turn the furrowed plain.
> Here the bright crocus and blue violet glow,
> Here Western winds on breathing roses blow.
>
> [Eclogue I]

Then he tells Daphnis that he is going to look after the lambs and the oxen and watch their dancing shadow when they run or frisk. Daphnis takes a decorated bowl. There are ivy creepers and grape vines painted beautifully on its surface. Within the creepers there are the figures of the four seasons: "Four figures rising from the work appear,/ The various seasons of the rolling year." He also refers to the signs of Zodiac.

> And what is that, which binds the radiant sky,
> Where twelve fair signs in beauteous order lie?
>
> [Eclogue I]

The twelve fair signs are Aries, Taurus, Gemini, Cancer, Leo, Virgo, Libra, Scorpio, Sagittarius, Capricorn, Aquarius and Pisces. The reference to the signs of Zodiac indicates that Pope like Chaucer was interested in astrology.

Damon hears their speeches and then advises them to sing by turns. It is to be noticed that his speech too is equally replete with references to the beauty of nature.

> Now hawthorns blossom, now the daisies spring,
> Now leaves the trees, and flowers adorn the ground;
> Begin, the vales shall every note rebound.
>
> [Eclogue I]

Here Milton's influence is quite obvious. Milton was fond of using inversions, Keats said that he left *Hyperion* unfinished because there were too many Miltonic inversions. Pope has used inversion judiciously. Here the inversion in the line "Now leaves the trees, and flowers adorn the ground" is used for brevity of expression.

Love is the other theme of the poem. Strephon sings about his beloved Delia:

Inspire me, Phoebus, in my Delia's praise,
With Waller's strains, or Granville's moving lays!
A milk white bull shall at your altars stand
That threats a fight, and spurns the rising sand.

[Eclogue I]

Phoebus is the sun god and patron of poetry. Strephon invokes him for inspiration. Then he remembers the well-known Elizabethan poet Edmund Waller famous for his love songs and George Granville, afterwards Lord Lansdowne, known for his poems, most of which he composed very young, and considered Waller his model. He again comes to the altar of Phoebus where the white bull made of marble is placed.

Now is the turn of Daphnis whose beloved is Sylvia.

O Love! for Sylvia let me gain the prize,
And make my tongue victorious as her eyes:
No lamb or sheep for victims I'll impart
Thy victim, Love, shall be the shepherd's heart.

[Eclogue I]

Even at the young age of sixteen, Pope was able to use wit commandingly. The wit in the last two lines is praiseworthy. Both the swains continue their dialogue singing the glory of the spring season and the intensity of their love. Strephon tells how innocent his beloved Delia is:

My gentle Delia beckons from the plain,
Then hid in shades, eludes her eager swain;
But feigns a laugh to see me search around,
And by that laugh the willing fair is found.

Daphnis' beloved Sylvia is as natural as Delia.

The sprightly Sylvia trips along the green,
She runs but hopes she does not run unseen,
While a kind glance at her pursuer flies,
How much at variance are her feet and eyes!

[Eclogue I]

These lines remind us of Keats's "Ode on a Grecian Urn" where the picture of a lover pursuing a maiden is carved. The difference between the two is that Daphnis' beloved runs but looks behind at her lover kindly. She is full of love for him and runs playfully without any intention to tease him.

Strephon shifts his focus from Delia to the beauty of the landscape:

> Over golden sand let rich Pactolus flow,
> And trees weep amber on the banks of Po;
> Bright Thames' shores the brightest beauties yield,
> Feed here, my lambs, I'll seek no distant field.
>
> [Eclogue I]

Here Pope has combined Italy and England together. Pactolus and Po are rivers of Italy and Thames of England. The classical references and Pope's indebtedness to Denham have been explained best by John Wilson Crocker, editor of the *Works*. He comments in the footnote to the poem:

> It is evident from the mention of the "golden sands" of Pactolus, and the "amber" of the poplars in connection with the Thames, that he had in view Denham's description in "Cooper's Hill".
>
> "Though with those streams he no resemblance hold,/ Whose foam is amber, and their gravel gold." The sisters of Phoeton, according to the classical fable, were, upon the death of their brother, turned into poplars on the banks of the Po, and the tears which dropt from these trees were said to be converted into amber.[6]

According to *Concise Oxford English Dictionary*, "Amber is a hard translucent fossilized resin originating from extinct coniferous trees, typically yellowish in colour and used in jewellery."[7]

As the beauty of the place is enchantingly arresting, he decides to stay there and see his lambs grazing and playing leisurely. Daphnis, like Strephon, combines the beauty of Italy with that of England.

Celestial Venus Haunts Idalia's groves;
Diana Cynthus, Ceres Hyble loves;
If Windsor-shades delight the matchless maid,
Cynthus and Hybia yield to Windsor-shade.

[Eclogue I]

Strephon makes a hyperbolic statement that his beloved's smile can brighten the sad nature of winter and usher in the mirthful spring season.

All nature mourns, the skies relent in showers
Hushed are the birds, and closed the drooping flowers;
If Delia smiles, the flowers begin to spring
The skies to brighten, and the birds to sing.

[Eclogue I]

Daphnis is not behind him in praising the joyful effect of Sylvia.

All nature laughs, the groves are fresh and fair,
The sun's mild lustre warms the vital air;
If Sylvia smiles, new glories gild the shore
And vanquished nature seems to charm no more.

[Eclogue I]

Strephon expresses his loyalty to Delia and says that his love of nature varies from time to time but his love for Delia is constant. He loves the flower covered fields in the spring season, the snowclad mountains in the autumn, the plains coloured golden in the morning by the rays of the sun and the cool shady groves in the noon hours in summer but Delia all the time. If she is absent from his sight nothing in nature can delight him. Daphnis tells of his love for Sylvia in a different way. He says that his Sylvia is like ripe autumn and wild like the month of May. She is brighter than the moon and as fresh as morning. Without her the spring season is listless and when she is with him there is the spring season in its full glory round the year.

Finally, Strephon challenges Daphnis in a new way.

Say, Daphnis, say, in what glad soil appears,
A wonderous tree that sacred monarchs bears;

Tell me but this, and I'll disclaim the prize
And give the conquest to thy Sylvia's eyes.

[Eclogue I]

The riddle is rather difficult for an ordinary Shepherd. The tree mentioned in the passage is the royal oak in which Charles II had been hid from the pursuit after the battle of Worcester. Daphnis does not answer the question rather poses a challenge, through a riddle alluding to the thistle worn by Queen Anne.

Nay tell me first, in what more happy fields
The thistle springs, to which the lily yields
And then a nobler prize I will resign;
For Sylvia, charming Sylvia shall be thine.

[Eclogue I]

Damon feels that both have crossed the limit. As an arbiter, he asks them to stop contention and enjoy the beauty of the reigning spring.

Cease to content; for Daphnis, I decree
The bowl to Strephon, and the lamb to thee.
Blest swains, whose nymphs in every grace excel
Blest nymphs, whose swains those graces sing so well.

[Eclogue I]

After praising all the four—Strephon, Delia, Daphnis and Sylvia—and blessing them for their sincere love, Damon describes the season's beauty in the most pleasant words:

Now rise, and haste to yonder woodbine bowers,
A soft retreat from sudden vernal showers;
The turf with rural dainties shall be crowned,
While opening blooms diffuse their sweets around.
For see! the gathering flocks to shelter tend,
And from the Pleiads fruitful showers descend.

[Eclogue I]

The second section titled "Summer" or "Alexis" is presented to Dr. Samuel Garth, author of the *Dispensary* and Pope's lifelong friend. The scene of this pastoral by the river side is suitable to the heat of the season at the noontime. This section is not in the form of eclogue, it is a simple narration but charged with feeling. The first ten lines are about a Shepherd's boy whose name is not given.

A Shepherd's boy (he seeks no better name)
Led forth his flocks along the silver Thame.
Where dancing sun-beams on the waters played
And Verdant alders formed a quivering shade.

[Eclogue II : Summer]

Since the waves of the river are going up and down under the force of the wind, the rays of the sun are described as dancing upon them. This is a beautiful picture of the waving river on a glittering day. However, as it has been pointed out by critics, Pope's description of the Shepherd's boy and the Thames is not original. He has imitated Edmund Spenser largely. The opening lines of Spenser's "Shepherd's Calendar" are:

A Shepherd boy (no better do him call)
Led forth his flock.

In fact, this section is ostensibly an imitation of Spenser's first eclogue which is devoted to a lover's complaint. The next six lines of "Summer" describe the sad heart of the Shepherd's boy:

Soft as he mourned, the streams forgot to flow,
The flocks around a dumb compassion show,
The Naiads wept in every watery bower
And Jove consented in a silent shower.

[Eclogue II]

After describing the sad heart of the Shepherd and nature's empathy, he addresses Dr. Garth and offers him the pastoral of the summer. If the first section is more about the beauty of nature, this section is solely devoted to love with some description of the summer season.

The beginning is rather gloomy. The words "mourned", "dump compassion", "wept" and "silent shower" indicate a gloomy environment, an environment where there is silence and sadness and even weeping is almost soundless. The poet addresses his friend Dr. Garth to listen to the sad music of love:

> Hear what from love unpracticed hearts endure
> From love, the sole disease though caust not cure.
>
> [Eclogue II]

In line number 25 the Shepherd declares his name that he is Alexis. But before that he has poured out his heart.

> Ye shady beeches, and ye cooling streams
> Defence from Phoebus', not from Cupid's beams,
> To you I mourn; not to the deaf I sing
> The woods shall answer, and their echo ring.
>
> [Eclogue II]

He is hopeful that the woods, the hills, the rocks and the bleating sheep will share his sorrow. It is a sad experience that the sultry Sirius is burning but his heart is frozen as if the winter season is reigning eternally. He invokes the nine muses to inspire him to write his feelings in a song or poem. He deplores his sad plight first:

> In those fair fields where sacred Isis glides
> Or else where Cam his winding vales divide
> As in the crystal stream I view my face
> Fresh rising blushes paint the watery glass
> But since those graces please thy eyes no more
> I shun the fountains which I sought before.
>
> [Eclogue II]

Here the contrast is obvious. The Shepherd used to sit by the river Cam gliding calmly and see his reflection in the clear water. But those days are gone. In the absence of his beloved, he feels no charm in this world and has stopped all his past activities. The change in him is really sad.

> Once I was skilled in every herb that grew,
> And every plant that drinks the morning dew;
> Ah wretched shepherd, what avails thy art,
> To cure thy lambs, but not to heal thy heart.
>
> [Eclogue II]

His sorrow is so deep and painful that he decides to leave the company of his fellow swains to do their everyday work like feeding their sheep or shearing their wool and then will sing his mournful songs about his love, sitting on the top of the nearby hill.

The flute he has in his hand was given by Colin, a poet who played on it and before his death bequeathed it to him. While handing over the flute, Colin told him that he sang about his beloved Rosalinda on that flute. Now he, Alexis, has that flute and will sing his sad songs, like a prisoned bird, in the bower.

Now he starts singing his song on the flute. Though he sings a mournful song, all the creatures of the forest listen to him attentively and feel great pleasure.

And yet my numbers please the rural throng
Rough satyrs dance, and Pan applauds the song
The nymphs, forsaking every care and spring
Their early fruit, and milk white turtles bring.

[Eclogue II]

The song changes the entire atmosphere; all that was sad and morose is now metamorphosed into joy and hilarity. The beauty of the summer season envelopes the valley with all its splendour. He tells his fellowmen that he will make a garland of dainty flowers and offer that garland of beauties to them gladly because they comprise all the beauties of nature. Then he describes the beauty of the summer season. The pictorial quality of these lines is remarkable.

See what delights in sylvan scene appear!
Descending gods have found Elysium here,
In Woods bright Venus with Adonis strayed;
And chaste Diana haunts the forest shade.
Come lovely nymph, and bless the silent hours
When swains from shearing seek their nightly bowers
When weary reapers quit the sultry field,
And crowned with corn their thanks to Ceres yield.

[Eclogue II]

But the reference to Venus and Adonis reminds him of his beloved Delia. He now feels the pangs of love and a strong desire to meet her. He says:

> This harmless grove no lurking viper hides,
> But in my breast the serpent love abides.
> Here bees from blossoms sip the rosy dew
> But your Alexis knows no sweets but you.

[Eclogue II]

Here Pope has used the word "sweets" in the early seventeenth century sense meaning "Perfume". The contrast between the love lorn heart of Alexis and the joyful nature is highlighted here. He remembers his beloved with poignance.

> Wherever you walk, cool gales shall fan the glade;
> Trees, where you sit, shall crowd into a shade;
> Wherever you tread, the blushing flowers shall rise
> And all things flourish where you turn your eyes.
> O! how I long with you to pass my days,
> Invoke the muses, and resound your praise!

[Eclogue II]

He imagines that his invocation will change the entire atmosphere. The birds shall sing the glory of their love and winds will carry it to all the corners of the country. He further says that she, too, will sing in the sweetest voice. Her song will be as sweet as that of the legendary Greek musician Orpheus. Hearing her song the forest will dance again gleefully. The song is so powerful that the mountains and the rivers will forget their nature. The immovable mountains will move and the running rivers will stand still to hear the sweet strain.

> The moving mountains hear the powerful call
> And headlong streams hang listening in their fall.

[Eclogue II]

While Alexis is pouring down the grief of his heart, the sun begins to decline. The shepherds who were taking rest in the shade of trees, leave the cool place and come out in the sun. The cows and oxen go to the brooks to quench their thirst. The flocks of sheep and lambs go back to their enclosures. In short, all objects go to their places of rest but, alas! there is no respite for him: "Ye gods! and is there no relief for love?" He looks at the setting sun going down the cooling sea but the flame of his love remains unextinguished.

> But soon the sun with milder rays descends
> To the cool ocean, where his journey ends
> On me love's fiercer flames for ever prey
> By night he scorches, as he burns by day.
>
> [Eclogue II]

With these lines the Shepherd's lament ends. Although this section is considered to be the weakest of the four the pictorial beauty and Alexis' romanticism are in the tradition of Virgil, Theocritus and Spenser. Pope's use of the line "The lowing herds to murmuring brooks retreat" was used by Thomas Gray in the second line of the first stanza of "Elegy Written in a Country Churchyard".

The third section titled "Autumn" or "Hylas and Aegon" is dedicated to William Wycherley, one of the leading playwrights of the Restoration period. Pope writes about him:

> Mr. Wycherley, a famous author of comedies; of which the most celebrated were the *Plain Dealer* and *Country Wife*. He was a writer of infinite spirit, satire and wit. The only objection made to him was, that he had too much. However, he was followed in the same way by Mr. Congreve, though with a little more correctness.[8]

This section is not a proper eclogue. Of course, Hylas and Aegon are speakers but they do not vie with each other as Strephon and Daphnis do in the first section. Besides, both characters speak only once. They are introduced in the opening lines:

> Beneath the shade a spreading beech displays
> Hylas and Aegon sung their rural lays;
> This mourned a faithless, that an absent love,
> And Delia's name and Doris' filled the grove.
>
> [Eclogue III: Autumn]

In a very subtle way their beloveds' names are given in the last line. We come to know that Delia is Hylas's beloved and Doris that of Aegon. Secondly, Hylas and Aegon do not address the people; on the other hand, it is the poet who narrates their tale. He invokes the deities to give him the power to tell the love-laden hearts of the two swains:

Thou whom the nine, with Plautus wit inspire,
The art of Terence, and Menander's fire;
Whose sense instructs us and whose humour charms,
Whose judgement sways us, and whose spirit warms!
Oh, skilled in nature! see the hearts of swains,
Their artless passion, and their tender pains.

[Eclogue III]

Here the words "the nine" mean the nine muses, patrons of poetry. Plautus, Terence and Menander are the famous classical poets. Here, Pope invokes the nine muses to inspire him to write about the naive passion of Hylas and Aegon. The phrase "artless passion" occurs with modification in "Elegy Written in a Country Churchyard" where the village poet relates the "artless tale" of the people buried in the Churchyard. After the invocation, he begins telling the love story of the swains.

It is afternoon. The sun is shining brightly. The clouds which look like the fleece of a sheep have become purple in colour because of the mild rays of the sun. It is at this hour that Hylas has started his mournful song of love, a song so moving that it makes the hard rocks weep and immovable mountains moan. The next six lines are written in the pattern of Edmund Waller's "Go Lovely Rose". The first stanza of Waller's poem is quoted here to show Pope's indebtedness to him:

Go, lovely rose,
Tell her that wastes her time and me,
That now she knows
When I resemble her to thee
How sweet and fair she seems to be.[9]

Pope's lines are:

Go gentle gales, and bear my sighs away

To Delia's ear the tender notes convey
As some sad turtle his lost love deplores
And with deep murmurs fills the sounding shores
Thus far from Delia, to the winds I mourn
Alike unheard, unpitied, and forlorn.

[Eclogue III]

Pope, however, has changed the mood. Waller is sad but hopeful; his heart is not broken, but Hylas is sad and his heart broken. It seems he has lost all hopes. The next stanza continues the same pensive mood. He requests the wind to carry his message to Delia that birds, "the feathered quires" have stopped singing, the lime trees have shed their leaves, the lily flowers are drooping and dying, and the leaves are fading fast because of her absence. Her absence has made the entire landscape dull and dry. He sends the message through the gales that he is eagerly waiting for her and her absence is too painful for him.

Go, gentle gales, and bear my sighs along!
The birds shall cease to tune their evening song,
The winds to breathe, the waving woods to move,
And streams to murmur, ere I cease to love.

[Eclogue III]

The final stanza ends with a happy note. Delia comes to him before the gales convey his message.

Go gentle gales, and bear my sighs away!
Come, Delia, come; ah, why this long delay?
Through rocks and caves the name of Delia sounds,
Delia, each cave and echoing rock rebounds.
Ye powers, what pleasing frenzy soothes my mind!
Do lovers dream, or is my Delia kind?
She comes! my Delia comes! Now cease my lay
And cease, ye gales, to bear my sighs away!

[Eclogue III]

Though Hylas' song is full of poignance, it fails to reach the height of Waller's song in melody and smoothness of flow. Waller's poem is a kind of *carpe diem* like the *Rubayats* of Omar

Khayyam or Andrew Marvell's "To His Coy Mistress"; Pope's poem is in the classical tradition and it would have been better if he had refrained from using the heroic couplet.

After Hylas' song is the song of Aegon. He is not lucky like Hylas. His voice resounds in the hills but Doris never replies. The poet is full of sympathy for him and invokes the muses to empower him with poetic power to express the anguish of Aegon's heart. He also requests the hills to resound his voice so that Doris can hear his complaint.

> Rehearse, ye muses, what yourselves inspired.
> Resound, ye hills, resound my mournful strain!
> Of perjured Doris, dying I complain.
>
> [Eclogue III]

It is going to be twilight. The day's work is ending and now it is the time that both lovers should meet but Doris does not come to Aegon. The twilight scene is beautifully described in these lines:

> While labouring oxen, spent with toil and heat,
> In their loose traces from the field retreat:
> While curling smokes from village tops are seen,
> And the fleet shades glide o'er the dusky green.
>
> [Eclogue III]

The arrival of darkness after the sunset makes the lover gloomy and he, now, makes his complaint in the most intense words. He remembers the pleasures they had in the past.

> Beneath yon poplar oft we passed the day:
> Oft on the rind I carved her amorous vows,
> While she with garlands hung the bending boughs.
>
> [Eclogue III]

But those happy games are no more played. The jilted lover mourns:

> The garlands fade, the vows are worn away;
> So dies her love, and so my hopes decay.
>
> [Eclogue III]

He looks at the nature around him. Things change in nature but they return again to their old forms, alas, her love which is now dead is not reviving.

Now bright Arcturus glads the teeming grain
Now golden fruits on loaded branches shine,
And grateful clusters swell with floods of wine;
Now blushing berries paint the yellow grove;
Just Gods! shall all things yield returns but love?

[Eclogue III]

This is a beautiful picture of the autumn season, the season of mellow fruitfulness. The use of the words "golden" and "yellow" indicates that the season is of the ripeness of crops, fruits and flowers. Pope has made use of juxtaposition and contrast to show the frustration of Aegon. His anguish intensifies further in the next stanza. He has now no desire to look after the sheep. If they become a prey to wild animals, he has no care for their life. He is exasperated that he himself has become a prey of his beloved's faithlessness. He laments:

Ah! what avails it me the flocks to keep,
Who lost my heart while I preserved my sheep?

[Eclogue III]

He resolves in desperation:

I'll fly from shepherds, flocks and flowery plains,
From shepherds, flocks and plains, I may remove,
Forsake mankind, and all the world—but love!

[Eclogue III]

Finally, he bids adieu to everything and decides to commit suicide by jumping from the top of the hill nearby.

Farewell, ye woods, adieu the light of day!
One leap from yonder cliff shall end my pains,
No more, ye hills, no more resound my strains!

[Eclogue III]

This speech is the speech of a person desperate in love. It also leads us to the gloom of wintry dark. After Aegon's speech there are only four lines that end the poem leading us to the winter season:

> Thus sang the shepherds till the approach of night
> The skies yet blushing with departing light
> When falling dews with spangles decked the glade
> And the low sun had lengthened every shade.
>
> [Eclogue III]

The title of the fourth section is winter or Daphne. It is written in memory of Mrs. Tempest. Pope writes about the lady:

> This lady was of ancient family in Yorkshire, and particularly admired by the author's (Pope's) friend Mr. Walsh, who having celebrated her in a Pastoral Elegy, desired his friend to do the same, as appears from one of his letters, dated Sept. 9, 1706. "Your last Eclogue being on the same subject with mine on Mrs. Tempest's death, I should take it very kindly in you to give it a little turn, as if it were to the memory of the same lady." Her death having happened on the night of the great storm in 1703, gave a propriety to this Eclogue, which in its general turn alludes to it. The scene of the Pastoral lies in a grove, the time at midnight.[10]

This pastoral is quite different from the rest. Love and the beauty of nature are the main themes in the first three. There is joy and happiness in "Spring" and "Summer". The third pastoral "Autumn" is a mixture of joy and sorrow. Hylas is happy because his beloved unites him but Aegon is drowned in sorrow. Autumn is the season of ripeness but it also ushers in the dreary winter. Aegon's lamentation is lost in darkness. Winter, which is the last phase of the cycle of seasons, is dark and dreary in Europe. Clouds, rains and hailstorms made people gloomy in the eighteenth century. This is why winter is usually associated with death and the spring season with birth.

"Winter" mourns the death of Mrs. Tempest who is called Daphne. Pope has heavily drawn on Theocritus and Bion. He is equally influenced by John Milton and his famous elegy *Lycidas*.

Here Lycidas and Thyrsis are the speakers who pay a glowing tribute to the deceased Mrs. Tempest.

Lycidas, a youth considered to be the handsomest man of the time, figured first in Virgil's eclogues. Later, John Milton made him the main character in the pastoral elegy to mourn the death of Edward King, his friend at Cambridge University. Thyrsis is the other handsome young man who has figured in many poems written during the classical period of Italy. These two characters mourn the death of Daphne who had a pastoral existence and who was futilely pursued by Apollo. She became a laurel tree and Apollo made a garland of the laurel leaves and wore it.

The first speaker is Lycidas. He asks Thyrsis to sing of Daphne's beauty and her tragic end. He says that the reason for making this request is that there is nothing on this earth which can match the sadness of his voice.

> Thyrsis, the music of that murmuring spring
> Is not so mournful as the strains you sing;
> Nor rivers winding through the vales below,
> So sweetly warble, or so smoothly flow.
>
> [Eclogue IV: Winter]

As the winter has set in, the time is midnight, the sheep are sleeping silently and the moon in serene glory is moving up the zenith of the sky, it is the fittest time for him to sing a mournful song. Thyrsis accepts the suggestion and then asks Lycidas to look at the desolate winter night.

> Behold the groves that shine with silver frost,
> Their beauty withered, and their verdure lost.
>
> [Eclogue IV]

After this he says that he will sing a mournful song as did Alexis:

> Here I shall I try the sweet Alexis' strain
> That called the listening dryads to the plain?
> Thames heard the numbers as he flowed along,
> And bade his willows learn the moving song.
>
> [Eclogue IV]

Lycidas, then, requests him to sing about Daphne's death as she was a great patron of the shepherds and her departure has hurt the shepherds. While Thyrsis is making preparations of his song, Lycidas will mourn at her tomb. Thyrsis, in the true classical tradition, invokes the muses to help him in his song. He requests them to leave the Pierian spring where water as clear as crystal flows and do what they did after Adonis' death. In other words, they inspired Bion to write an elegy on his death and, so, now they should help him to write a verse in memory of Daphne. In the meantime, the sky is overcast with gloomy clouds and trees are bending under the weight of pearly frost. The beauty of nature is declining after Daphne's death.

> For her the flocks refuse their verdant food
> Their thirsty heifers shun the gliding flood
> The silver swans her hapless fate bemoan,
> In notes more sad than when they sing their own.
>
> [Eclogue IV]

The stanza ends with the couplet:

> Her name with pleasure once she taught the shore,
> Now Daphne's dead, and pleasure is no more.
>
> [Eclogue IV]

The last line functions as refrain to each stanza of the poem. Thyrsis continues his song.

Now dews are not falling from the sky as they are stunned at Daphne's death. The flowers are not emitting their morning odour. The orchards are without the sweet smell of ripe fruits. The sweet smelling zephyr is silent. The ever busy honey bees have stopped their work of collecting honey. All the works of nature have come to standstill because "Fair Daphne's dead, and sweetness is no more".

When Daphne was alive, she sang so sweet songs that the skylarks suspended their wings in the air. The singing birds used to copy her sweet voice but now after her death they have stopped singing. The flowing streams murmurred to her singing. After her death, they have become silent. The stanza ends this way:

But tell the reeds, and tell the vocal shore,
Fair Daphne's dead, and music is no more.

[Eclogue IV]

Thyrsis tells that the whole world, that is his world, is mourning her death. The gentle breeze whispers that she is dead. The trees listen to the whispering voice in silence. The silvery stream is overwhelmed with grief and is shedding tears in grief.

The winds, and trees, and floods, her death deplore,
Daphne, our grief! our glory now no more.

[Eclogue IV]

But as the tradition of elegy is, no poem ends with tears in eyes. It ends with an optimistic note. Here, too, Thyrsis does not end his mourning with tearful eyes. He sees Daphne's spirit ascending towards heaven and reaching the place of eternal bliss.

But see! where Daphne wandering mounts on high
Above the clouds, above the starry sky!
Eternal beauties grace the shining scene,
Fields ever fresh, and groves for ever green!
There while you rest in amaranthine bowers,
Or from those meads select unfading flowers,
Behold us kindly, who your name implore
Daphne our goddess! and our grief no more!

[Eclogue IV]

Thus, Thyrsis ends his speech. Lycidas, who is tremendously moved by Thyrsis' lamentation, tells about its effect on him and the world around him, that every object of nature is hushed in silence with grief. He then hopes that Daphne's name shall be remembered for ever by all.

To thee, bright goddess, oft a lamb shall bleed,
If teeming ewes increase my fleecy breed.
While plants their shade, or flowers their odours give,
Thy name, thy honour, and thy praise shall live!

[Eclogue IV]

Thus, the elegy ends. Now Thyrsis looks around him. The winter is on. The sky looks threatening. He advises Lycidas to leave the place immediately.

> But see, Orien sheds unwholesome dews:
> Arise; the pines a noxious shade diffuse;
> Sharp Boreas blows, and nature feels decay,
> Time conquers all, and we must time obey.
>
> [Eclogue IV]

After this he bids farewell to all—the valleys, the mountains, the streams, the groves, the shepherds' country songs, his sheep, the sylvan woods and finally Daphne:

> Adieu you vales, ye mountains, streams and groves
> Adieu ye shepherds' rural lays and loves;
> Adieu my flocks; farewell, ye sylvan crew
> Daphne, farewell; and all the world adieu.
>
> [Eclogue IV]

Pope has written that:

> These four last lines allude to the several subjects of the Pastorals, and to the several scenes of them particularized before in each.

The editor of the *Works of Alexander Pope*, John Wilson Crocker, does not agree with the poet. He refutes him and makes the following comment:

> They should have been added by the poet in his own person, instead of being put into the mouth of a shepherd who is not presumed to have any knowledge of the previous pieces. The specific character which Pope ascribes to each of his Pastorals is not borne out by the poems themselves. There is as much about "flocks" in the first Pastoral as in the second; and there is as much about "rural lays and loves" in the second Pastoral as in the first. The third Pastoral contains no mention of a "sylvan crew", but a couple of shepherds are absorbed by the same "rural lays and loves" which occupied their predecessors.[11]

Dr. Crocker is quite right in his criticism. But we have to remember the fact that Pope wrote the Pastorals at the young age of sixteen and at that time he was not mature enough to take everything in account. Professor Dustin H. Griffin is more correct in his estimation of the Pastorals. He writes:

> The notice (and reminder) that the poems were written at age sixteen acts as a plea both for lenient judgement (these tepid things are but juvenilia) and greater admiration (these fine things were written by a mere boy). We are clearly encouraged to read the poems as highly contrived performances by a poet who quite consciously limited himself to certain effects....
>
> Thyrsis concludes his song, and Pope concludes the sequence. We do not need his 1736 note to see that "these four last lines allude to the several subjects of the four Pastorals, and to the several scenes of them". Behind Thyrsis we hear perhaps the young, sophisticated, self-limiting poet, whose restraint intimates great reserves of maturing strength. Having demonstrated his skill in pastorals, he bids it a master's farewell.[12]

Pope has followed the classical and Elizabethan concept of nature. In the "Pastorals" he is not different from Waller, Spenser and Marlowe. For him nature means the nature people commonly believe. He looks at the changes in nature with the cycle of seasons. The characters are simple shepherds who live in nature and are guided by nature. The beauty of the spring and the summer are skilfully depicted and the feelings and emotions generated by autumn and winter are aptly described. Besides, Pope is a kind of romanticist. The love-tormented hearts of Strephon, Daphnis, Alexis, Hylas and Aegon are not very much different from those of Spenser, Sidney, Marlowe, and the nineteenth century poets. It will be pertinent to quote Professor G. Wilson Knight's views:

> Pope's early instincts were pastoral.... What is pastoral? Pastoral normally envisages man in a sunny climate at work which appears to be limited to the comparatively easy business of guarding and caring for one's flocks: life is, or appears, simple. But is this necessarily a release? No, for now we are faced only the more clearly by the basic torments of life: love and death, unreachable desire

> and irreparable loss. The pastoral—you feel it in Lyly's plays—defines the problems and tensions awaiting man when, if ever, all other turmoils are stilled. Of Pope's four early pastorals, the two best, summer and winter, are concerned respectively with love and death.
>
> Nature is one solution; poetry the other. In pastoral there is not only the obvious poetry. The *dramatis personae* are themselves poets, and engage in poetic competitions. In balancing man against nature, love against death, season with season, in the antiphonal speeches of the persons, and the techniques of the poetry itself, in all this we can say that pastoral is attempting to create a balance, or poise, in despite of, indeed composed of, man's most ultimate pains and problems.[13]

Pope at the young age of sixteen saw nature, man and poetry. What he aimed at was a co-ordination and harmony. As the existing concept of nature and art was unable to bring harmony, or what Knight says peace, he studied more and resorted to the new concept of nature and universe as interpreted by contemporary science and philosophy. His poetic theory came into practice first in *Windsor Forest* incoherently but perfectly in the later poems.

II

The next poem that Pope wrote is a product of his maturing period. *Windsor Forest* like the first pastoral "Spring" is a tribute to Sir William Trumble who patronized Pope and who himself was a man of wide learning and fine taste. It will be pertinent to see the development of Pope's mind before analysing the poem. The fact is that he was able to assimilate the eighteenth century concept of man, nature and art. Before him were two great masters: John Dryden and Henry Fielding. Both the writers believed that the world was an order built by God. Professor Battestin has shown the similarity in the ideas of Dryden and Henry Fielding.

"As England's Augustan Age began, Dryden somewhat extravagantly congratulated his friend Sir Robert Howard on the formal perfection of his poetry, which like the creation itself, was the product not of accident, but of art:

> ...this is a piece too fair
> To be the child of chance, and not of care.
> No atoms casually together hurled
> Could ever produce so beautiful a world.
> Nor dare I such a doctrine here admit,
> As would destroy the providence of wit.

As the age that Dryden inaugurated drew to a close, Henry Fielding applied the same bold metaphor to Tom Jones, declaring the coherence and integrity of his own 'great creation', which he had carefully contrived and over which he presided, omniscient and unerring."[14]

This long quotation from Professor Battestin's *Providence of Wit* makes it amply clear that the poetic theory and practice of the eighteenth century united the orderliness in God's creation with the poetic form.

Windsor Forest, finally completed in 1713, is an attempt at looking at nature as a system created by God. It, too, is pastoral in form but at a different level. The humble pastoral singer follows Milton's "Groves of Eden". Though Pope in the prefatory notes says that the poem is about Windsor Forest and its green retreats, he goes beyond the conventions of the pastoral. Griffin comments:

> *Windsor Forest* (1713) more clearly presents an apparently similar case [of Aegon in "Winter": pastoral humility signals the confidence of the role player who could do more if he would.... The poem strains at the bounds of rural-descriptive verse to encompass prophecy of England's future greatness and celebration of Windsor's royal heroes.[15]

The poem begins with a deep submission to nature and later on expands into communal and national prophecy. The forest is a universal symbol.

> Thy Forests, Windsor! and thy Green Retreats,
> At once the Monarch's and the Muse's seats.[16] (1-2)

Here, we see that the poem in spite of its pastoral setting is a symbol of England. Professor G. Wilson Knight considers the Windsor Forest a universal symbol. He quotes lines 10-13 of the poem:

> Not chaos-like together crushed and bruised,
> But as the world, harmonious confused:
> Where order in variety we see
> And where, though all things differ, agree. (10-13)

Then he comments:

> Those four lines, balancing man and nature with feeling for an enclosing and permeating whole, are the key to Pope's work.[17]

Nobody will refute Professor Knight's interpretation but it is also that Pope looks at Windsor Forest "nature as art". The first line reminds us of Genesis when there was chaos. God created this universe out of chaos. This world is a creation of God. The forest which is nature and which is God's creation is a work of art where there is order in variety and the warring elements are in harmony.

The poem then proceeds to a formal description of the forest's order in variety:

> There, interspersed in lawns and opening glades,
> Thin trees arise that shun each other's shades. (20-21)

Here, as Knight has interpreted, the class nouns—lawns, glades, trees and shades—balance a vivid feeling for natural life. He draws our notice to the use of personification in these lines and the lines that follow them.

> Notice that the personification of the trees is not a weak artifice: rather their felt stillness, their living identities, are realized. Personification in Pope is never driven to any rigid extremes. When corn is seen in waving prospect (39) we have movement and a whole, steady scene, together with an abstract noun: and all movement, wholeness, and the abstract well used in service to a physical impact, are characteristic.[18]

The poem then makes a historical survey of Windsor's Norman past in lines 43 to 92. After that follows a beautiful account of hunting scenes. These lines are remarkable for their lively description. Here is the flower with his gun:

He lifts the tube, and levels with his eye:
Straight a short thunder breaks the frozen sky:
Oft as in airy rings they skim the heath,
The clamorous lapwings feel the leaden death:
Oft, as the mounting larks their notes prepare,
They fall, and leave their little lives in air. (124-29)

Pope is really moved at the killing of the birds. But he does not sentimentalize the scene. The last line very calmly states the tragic fall of the birds when they are shot dead. It is a quality of Pope that he is never sentimental. The visual imagery is superb.

The focus shifts from the hunting scenes to the metamorphosis of Lodona into a local stream. According to the Greek mythology Pan pursued Lodona, a beautiful maiden. Lodona ran away from him and cried for help. The gods transmuted her to a small stream. Now,

The silver stream her virgin coldness keeps,
For ever murmurs, and for ever weeps. (204-05)

By introducing the myth of Pan and Lodona, Pope has brought in the element of human activity in Windsor Forest. Professor Knight in his analysis of the poem comments that Pope, at first, looks at nature and then the animals. Once the animals are mentioned, man enters the forest. Knight explains the animal imagery and then the human activity and the importance of the Lodona myth in the poem:

> Animals are usually created in their vital and peculiar movement from an inward sympathy comparable with Shakespeare's and continuous with the apprehension of dynamic quality, as well as shape and colour, in nature generally.[19]

He quotes lines 118-20 and says that the stallion and hare of Shakespeare's *Venus and Adonis* are both recalled by Windsor

Forest. There is the recognition of the animal behaviour in the poem. His explanation that there is a pattern in nature and that animals and human beings follow that pattern cannot be disputed. We quote this long passage from *The Laureate of Peace* which explains the validity of the Lodona myth in the poem.

> Such recognition will naturally widen beyond nature animal life to a vivid feeling for human vitality in action, such as we find in Pan's pursuit of Lodona (171-218). A tense realization of movement and fear is projected through numerous precisions involving bold comparisons, the sound of steps, Pan's shadow lengthened by the sun, the feeling of his very breath: it is vivid without being visual, an inward experience expressing itself freely and variously; and it should help us to the understanding of Shakespeare's own similar mastery. The little drama leads upto Lodona's transmutation to a rivulet.... That process of nature-feeling which created the Greek myths, and which Keats understood so well in his own fluid personifications, enjoys an equal perfection here.[20]

After the Lodona myth Pope moves on to the human world. He looks at the river Thames, "great father of the British floods". There are "the lofty woods" and the "towering oaks" standing on its banks. They symbolise England's royal greatness. He hints at the importance of the Thames to the commercial nation:

> Not Neptune's self from all his streams receives
> A Wealthier tribute, than to thine he gives.
> No seas so rich, so gay no banks appear. (50-52)

He compares in a very subtle way the reign of Queen Elizabeth with that of Queen Anne. G. Wilson Knight has shown the parallelism between the two queens by referring to the history plays of Shakespeare. The Windsor Forest stands as a symbol of England in these lines:

> Nor envy Windsor! since thy shades have seen
> As bright a goddess, and as chaste a queen;
> Whose care, like [Diana's] protects the sylvan reign
> The earth's fair light, and empress of the main.
> (161-64)

A little later, Pope faces two choices: the courtly life and the retired life of a poet. First is the description of the courtly life:

Happy the man whom this bright court approves
His sovereign favours, and his country loves. (235-36)

We expect that he will continue to praise the glamorous world of the court. But, surprisingly, he turns away from the glamour and luxury of the courtly life.

Happy next him who to these shades retires,
Whom nature charms, and whom the muse inspires,
Whom humbler joys of home-felt quiet please
Successive study, exercise and ease. (237-40)

He continues for eighteen lines more, describing the activities at the retired man and his humbler joy. The final decision is in favour of the retired post.

Ye sacred Nine! that all my soul possess,
Whose raptures fire me, and whose visions bless,
Bear me, Oh bear me to sequestered scenes,
The bowery mazes and surrounding greens. (259-62)

Pope's real affinity, as he says in the quoted passage, is not with the political and commercial greatness, symbolized by the Thames, but with the virgin simplicity of Lodona, the small river flowing melodiously in the forest. Just as she shrinks from the dangerous glory of having strayed beyond the green forest, Pope, also shrinks from the pomp and glory of the court.

Finally, he thinks of the god-like poets who once sang in these shades, though now their voices have been stopped by fate. Perhaps, reluctant to offer himself as the obvious heir of Denham and Cowley, he asks:

Who now shall charm the shades where
Cowley strung His living harp?

and answers thus:

But hark! the groves rejoice, the forest rings!
Are these revived? or is it Granville sings?
'Tis yours, my Lord, to bless our soft retreats,
And call the Muses to their ancient seats,

To paint anew the flowery sylvan scenes,
To crown the forests with immortal greens,
Make Windsor Hills in lofty numbers rise,
And lift her turrets nearer to the skies;
To sing those honours you deserve to wear,
And add new lustre to her silver star. (281-90)

The "Silver star" is the poet himself who will shine with the blessings of the Nine Muses.

The 1704 edition of *Windsor Forest* ends here. Later on Pope expanded it. The reason for doing so is explained by Griffin:

> Why did Pope expand the poem by 144 lines in 1713? Perhaps, as the epigraph hints, because he was again "commanded: non injussa cano" ("Unbidden strains I sing not"). That the bidding again was Granville who is likewise there hinted: "'tis of thee, Varus [to whom Virgil's poem was dedicated] our tamarisk shall sing, of thee all our groves. To Phoebus no page is more welcome than that which bears on its front the name of Varus." Indeed one might fairly say that in the continuation of *Windsor Forest* Pope does "sing Granville" and make Granville (rather than himself) sing the glories of the peace.[21]

There is no break between the first version and the added 144 lines. Granville, who was bidden earlier to paint Windsor Forest's "sylvan scene", is now urged to sing of Windsor's heroes:

Oh wouldst thou sing what heroes Windsor bore,
What kings first breathed upon her winding shore,
Or raise old warriors whose adored remains
In weeping vaults her hallowed earth contains!
(299-302)

As already said, Pope, in the added lines, goes on to recall the glories of Windsor's Kings and warriors from Edward III to Charles I as an appropriate subject for poetry. He is humble enough to say that it is Granville's subject, not his own. He wants to follow Granville, his instructor. After this, he comes back to Father Thames. Griffin explains the significance of the Thames and the river imagery:

> The subsequent introduction of Father Thames marks a return to the mythological mode of the first version: "In that blest moment, from his oozy bed/ Old Father Thames advanced his reverend head." The Thames appears with his "seaborn brothers" around his throne, and Pope luxuriates in a brief river catalogue (lines 340-48), but Thames' real function is to serve as a symbol of England's commercial and political glory.[22]

The last sixty-five lines unfold England's glory. They are one of the most rapturous lines Pope ever wrote:

> Here Orpheus sings; trees moving to the sound
> Start from their roots, and form a shade around
> Amphion there the loud creating lyre
> Strikes, and behold a sudden Thebes aspire!
> Cythoeron's echoes answer to his call,
> And half the mountain rolls into a wall:
> There might you see the lengthening spires ascend,
> The Domes swell up, the widening arches bend,
> The growing towers like exhalations rise
> And the huge columns heave into the skies. (411-20)

Both in the *Pastorals* and in *Windsor Forest,* Pope has demonstrated his technique of the pastoral mode. The setting, the characters and the imagery make them perfect poems of nature. Nature, in the early years of Pope, was nature as it appeared before his predecessors and the romantics. We are led to the world of simple people, the shepherds, who live in the company of nature. The description of the different seasons—the blossoming of the spring, the luxuriance of the summer, the ripeness of the autumn and the melancholy of the winter—is all real and self-experienced. The *Windsor Forest*, in spite of its reference to the English history and the line of the monarchs, is basically a nature poem. Pope very rightly leaves for Granville the lofty subjects and chooses to write simple poems, as plain as the shepherds and as fresh as nature itself:

> My humble Muse, in unambitious strains
> Paints the green forests and the flowery plains.
> (427-28)

Notes

1. G. Wilson Knight, *Laureate of Peace* (London: Routledge & Kegan Paul, 1954), p. 3.
2. A. Pope, "A Discourse on Pastoral Poetry", *Works of Pope*, ed. J.W. Crocker (London: John Murray, 1971), p. 258.
3. *Idem.*
4. J.W. Crocker, "Pastorals", *The Poetical Works of Alexander Pope*, p. 265.
5. *Ibid.* "Notes".
6. *Ibid.*, p. 272.
7. *Concise Oxford English Dictionary* (1998), p. 41.
8. *Works of Alexander Pope*, p. 285.
9. *Palgraés Golden Treasury* (London: OUP, 1960), p. 251.
10. Pope, "Introduction", *Works of Alexander Pope*, p. 292.
11. John Wilson Crocker, "Footnotes", *Works of Alexander Pope*, p. 300.
12. Dustin H. Griffin, *Studies in Pope's Poetry* (Princeton: Princeton Univ. Press, 1974), p. 76.
13. G. Wilson Knight, *Laureate of Peace, On the Genius of Pope* (London: Routledge & Kegan Paul, 1954), pp. 166-67.
14. Martin S. Battestin, *The Providence of Wit* (London: OUP, 1974), p. 1.
15. Dustin H. Griffin, *Studies in Pope's Poetry*, p. 77.
16. *Works*, p. 75. All quotations are from *The Works of Alexander Pope*. The line numbers are given at the end.
17. G. Wilson Knight, *Laureate of Peace* (London: Routledge & Kegan Paul, 1954), p. 17.
18. *Ibid.*, pp. 17-18.
19. *Ibid.*, p. 20.
20. *Ibid.*, pp. 20-21.
21. Dustin H. Griffin, *Studies in Pope's Poetry*, p. 80.
22. *Ibid.*, p. 81.

3

Essay on Criticism

Essay on Criticism is Pope's first mature work. Though modelled after Horace's *Ars Poetica*, it is Pope's testament of poetic theory and practice. For Dryden and Fielding, the task of the creative writer was to follow God's design. Pope added nature. In his poetic theory, there is God and there is man and between the two is *nature*.

> First follow nature, and your judgement frame
> By her just standard, which is still the same.
> Unerring NATURE, still divinely bright,
> One clear, unchanged, and universal light.[1] (68-71)

Pope deviates from his predecessors and makes a fusion of nature and art. W.K. Wimsatt and Cleanth Brooks have explained Pope's concept of nature very lucidly:

> Nature (the object of artistic imitation) has, for Pope, three main features. First, Nature is a Platonic and Stoic Universal order and superior reality.
>
> Secondly, Nature the universal order, assimilates readily with man's effort to enforce or increase that order in his own affairs—that is, with his civilization and all its parts, his cities, institutions, business and recreations. Pope's nature is the nature not only of Windsor Forest, but also of Hampton, Stowe, Twickenham, Drury Lane, Button and Grubstreet. It is the nature of socially ordered

> human conduct. Its antithesis is eccentricity or hyper-individualism....
>
> Thirdly, Pope's idea of nature has the distinction of residing in a state of great harmony with the idea of the classical models. No other poet or theorist has expressed the reconciliation of these threateningly twin standards—the rivals, modern reason and classic authority—with such persuasive aplomb.[2]

In fact, Pope is the only poet of the eighteenth century who has synthesised the ideas of the classical period with those of his age, the age of reason. As has been seen in the previous chapter, he was avowedly a follower of Virgil, Theocritus and Spenser and saw nature in the way the Elizabethans did. But the spectacular aspect of nature, he found was not the reality nor, he sincerely felt, man should suffer from unrequited love. Heart has got its value but emotions must be controlled by reason. Pope found solution in God, nature and art.

Professor Battestin in the first chapter of his book *Providence of Wit* has discussed at length the current ideas of the eighteenth century and arrived at the conclusion that the idea of order in nature and art was not confined to poetry only but it extended to architecture, painting, music and even science. He cites the example of Kepler, one of the greatest astronomers of all time. He titles the chapter "The Idea of Order in Nature and the Arts 1660-1750" and divides it into two parts: (a) Nature as Art and (b) Art as the Imitation of Nature.

He expresses the view, and very rightly, that both *Essay on Criticism* and *An Essay on Man* should be read as two aspects of the same coin. In fact, both the poems are complementary to each other and when joined together they make a perfect whole. His succinct summary of Pope's view of nature, man and art is quoted here:

> Echoing Aristotle in *Essay on Criticism* (1711), Pope advised the poet to "First follow Nature" (l. 68); in *An Essay on Man* (1733-34), reducing the Christian humanist philosophy of order to an epigram, he defined that Nature which the Augustan artist believed he was imitating: "All

> Nature is but Art, unknown to thee; All Chance, Direction, which thou canst see."[3] (289-90)

The first quoted line from *Essay on Criticism* refers to the concept of poetry as imitation of nature and the next quoted lines from *An Essay on Man* to the concept of nature as art. We shall discuss the first concept while analysing the poem *Essay on Criticism* and the second concept in *An Essay on Man*.

II

Essay on Criticism was published in 1711 in its final form. But, as Professor Dobreé has pointed out, Pope began writing it in 1709. He writes:

> Though not published until 1711, and then anonymously, it appears to have been written in 1709;

It is amazing that Pope could write such a well-organized piece of criticism in verse at the young age of twenty-three. The incomplete sentence we have just quoted continues thus: "and the organizing power required to marshal, and to concentrate into less than 750 lines, the accumulated thought upon criticism of all the centuries since Aristotle, might easily fail a poet".[4]

Griffin writes about *Essay on Criticism*:

> It is a paradox that repeats itself in Pope's early
> verse: diffident poet and confident poem.[5]

In support of his remark he quotes Ripley Hotch:

> The poem has the bounce and go of verse by a terribly bright young man who has recently acquired all the right ideas, which he gets off with dazzling verbal skill and cheerful superiority.[6]

I too feel that Ripley Hotch is more balanced in his estimate that Pope, being a young poet, demonstrates humility in this poem and humility is an indispensable quality which every poet-critic should possess.

Pope, as Wimsatt and Brooks have pointed out, is highly influenced by Horace and his *Ars Poetica*. Horace has given judicious and practical advice to poets. So *Essay on Criticism* written in the style of the classical poet-critic, too, is a piece of advice to the poets and critics of the eighteenth century.

The first eight lines weigh the poet and the critic and favour the scale for the poet:

'Tis hard to say, if greater want of skill
Appear in writing or in judging ill;
But, of the two, less dangerous is the offence
To tire our patience, than mislead our sense.

[*Essay on Criticism*, 1-4]

Pope admits that a bad poet may bore the listeners but his offence or infirmity is pardonable when he is compared to a critic. The reason is that a bad critic will lead us astray. In the next six lines he furthers his point and says that a poet may make a mistake in his poem but the critic who writes prose, and it is much simpler to write in prose, makes several mistakes. Then he proceeds to say that both good poets and good critics are very rare.

Both must alike from heaven derive their light,
These born to judge, as well as those to write. (13-14)

He defends the arrogance of the poet who is partial to his wit and criticisms the critic who is proud of his judging ability. After this he gives his opinion on the relationship between nature, art and criticism.

Yet, if we look more closely, we shall find
Most have the seeds of judgment in their mind;
Nature affords at least a glimmering light,
The lines, though touched but faintly, are drawn aright.

(18-21)

Here, Pope is influenced by Joseph Addison who made the remark that only good poets could be good critics. Poets are guided by nature, the perfect balancing power, and imitate its principles of order and harmony. Since they are balanced in poetic composition they are balanced in their appraisal and make sound judgements while appreciating poetry written by others. After this he begins his onslaught on those critics who have failed as poets. These critics,

In search of wit, oft lose their common sense
And then turn critics in their own defence. (28-29)

He calls them fools and compares them with a minor poet who tries to spite Apollo in his verse. Their character is beautifully summarised in these witty lines:

Some have at first for wits, then poets passed
Turned critics next, and proved plain fools at last.
(36-37)

But a large majority of the so-called critics is worse:

Some neither can for wits nor critics pass,
As heavy mules are neither horse nor ass,
Those half learned witlings, numerous in our isle,
As half-formed insects on the banks of Nile;
Unfinished things, one knows not what to call,
Their generation's so equivocal. (38-43)

The image of the tadpoles (half-formed insects) reveals the sharpness of Pope's art of ridiculing his opponents.

After these preliminaries he describes the qualities of a good critic, in fact, the poet-critic. The prime quality of the critic is to "follow nature" or be naturally discreet.

But you who seek to give and merit fame,
And justly bear a critic's noble name
Be sure yourself and your own reach to know
How far your genius, taste, and learning go;
Launch not beyond your depth, but be discreet
And mark that point where sense and dullness meet.
(46-51)

Discretion and the ability to mark the line dividing wit and foolishness are the qualities of a critic. The question is: Wherefrom will he gain or learn these two qualities? The answer is that nature is the best source. Nature is perfect and it has set a limit to everything. Excess and shortage both are harmful.

Nature to all things fixed the limits fit,
And wisely curbed proud man's pretending wit. (52-53)

The excess of one thing leads to the shortage of the other. Therefore, everything should be kept in proper balance as does nature. He explains this idea with three examples, those of memory and understanding, of the advancing sea and the sand, and of the king who conquers new lands but becomes careless of the previously won lands.

> As on the land while here the ocean gains,
> In other parts it leaves wide sandy plains;
> Thus in the soul while memory prevails,
> The solid power of understanding fails. (54-57)

> Like kings we lose the conquests gained before
> By vain ambition still to make them more. (64-65)

The reason for recognizing our limits is that man is a finite being.

> One science only will one genius fit;
> So vast is art, so narrow human wit. (60-61)

Pope, then advises the critic to follow nature and base his judgement on its principles.

> First follow nature, and your judgement frame
> By her just standard which is still the same:
> Unerring nature, still divinely bright,
> One clear, unchanged, and universal light,
> Life, force, and beauty, must to all impart,
> At once the source, and end, and test of art. (68-73)

As the comments of Wimsatt and Brooks have already been quoted in reference to these lines, we can only add that they express best Pope's concept of art and nature. Nature is the source, end and test of art. It is the divine light which gives life, energy and beauty to all kinds of art.

When art follows nature, it becomes "methodised nature". Pope writes:

> Those rules of old discovered, not devised
> Are nature still, but nature methodised. (88-89)

Now the question is, what are those old rules? The answer is the balance between heart and head. As nature is orderly and systematic and its rules are specific to symmetry and harmony and maintain unity in variety, the poet too should be guided by reason to maintain a balance between wit and judgement.

> Some to whom heaven in wit has been profuse,
> Want as much more, to turn it to its use;
> For wit and judgement often are at strife,
> Though meant each other's aid, like man and wife.
>
> (80-83)

Pope compares wit to a horse that has to be restrained by its rider. Imagination must not be wild. The old rule is that the poet should always be guided by reason:

> 'Tis more to guide, than spur the muse's steed;
> Restrain his fury, than provoke his speed;
> The winged courser, like a generous horse,
> Shows more true mettle when you check his course.
>
> (84-87)

If wits follow nature they will realise the truth that nature, like liberty, is restrained. Liberty is not licence. If we want to maintain liberty and enjoy its blessings, we have to control ourselves and must not intrude upon the liberty of others. God made this world orderly and orderliness comes from the laws that discipline the movement of the heavenly bodies.

Pope refers to the classical Greece. The great Greek poets had the flight of imagination but they restrained it by reason. They followed nature and nature in turn made them great poets. The critics, too, followed nature. The result was great benefit for both the poet and the critic.

> The generous critic fanned the poets' fire,
> And taught the world with reason to admire
> Then criticism the muse's handmaid proved,
> To dress her charms, and make her more beloved.
>
> (100-03)

But those people who deviated from the true path became critics of the low class.

> But following wits from that intention strayed,
> Who could not win the mistress, wooed the maid;
> Against the poets their own arms they turned,
> Sure to hate most the men from whom they learned.
> (104-07)

It is really bad for the people of noble families to court their maid-servants when they are unable to woo a well-mannered lady born in a noble family. The editor of the *Works*, makes the following comments on these quoted lines:

> The entire passage seems to be constructed on some remarks of Dryden in his Dedication to Ovid: formerly the critics were quite another species of men. They were defenders of poets, and commentators on their works, to illustrate obscure beauties, to place some passages in a better light, to redeem others from malicious interpretations. Are our auxiliary forces turned our enemies? Are they from our seconds become principals against us?[7]

Pope compares the modern critics to apothecaries and poets to doctors. The doctors are learned people who know the nature of diseases and their prescriptions are of true value. But the half educated apothecaries take their prescriptions and use them indiscriminately.

> So modern apothecaries, taught the art
> By doctor's bills to play the doctor's part,
> Bold in the practice of mistaken rules,
> Prescribe, apply, and call their masters fools. (108-11)

The other kind of critics is worse.

> Some on the leaves of ancient authors prey
> Nor time nor moths o'er spoiled so much as they;
> Some dryly plain, without invention's aid,
> Write dull receipts how poems may be made
> These leave the sense, their learning to display,
> And those explain the meaning quite away. (112-17)

In short though they are unable to write good poetry, they advise others how to write poems. Just as apothecaries make a mess of a doctors' prescription, these critics destroy the original sense of the poem written by a poet. There is a quibble in the lines 113-15. Time and moths spoil books by destroying them; bad commentators spoil them by explaining them wrongly.

Pope advises his contemporaries to follow the norms of the classical age. If modern critics follow the old rules they will not cavil or fuss over petty matters.

> You then whose judgement the right course would steer,
> Know well each ancient's proper character;
> His fable, subject, scope in every page;
> Religion, country, genius of his age:
> Without all these at once before your eyes,
> Cavil you may, but never criticise. (118-23)

After this passage follow his famous lines:

> Be Homer's works your study and delight,
> Read them by day and meditate by night. (124-25)

It may be asked why Pope advises young poets to read Homer studiously and meditate on his art. The answer is that, to Pope, nature and art are the same in Homer's poetry.

> When first young Maro in his boundless mind
> A work to outlast immortal role designed
> Perhaps he seemed above the critic's law
> And but from nature's fountain scorned to draw:
> But when to examine every part he came
> Nature and Homer were, he found the same. (130-35)

It is clear here that Pope's intention is to show the inextricable relationship between nature and art. The last line of the passage means that Homer followed nature faithfully and his art is nature methodised. By nature methodised Pope means the adoption of the system of nature (order, balance and harmony in variety) in a literary work. His advice for the younger generation of poets is:

Learn hence for ancient rules a just esteem
To copy nature is to copy them. (139-40)

After stating the basic principle that God is perfect and nature which is a part of His vast design is perfect and that poetry must follow the system of nature to achieve perfection, Pope comes to the form of poetry. He says that the classical poets wrote their serious poetry in the heroic couplet, a stanza of two lines in iambic pentameter in which each line has a caesura which balances the two feet preceding it and the two feet that follow it. The movement is slow and majestic. There is regularity and harmony. Let us know that the rhyming of the two lines forming a couplet and the idea completed at the end of the second line is not specific to European poetry. In Persian, Urdu and Hindi poetry, rhyme plays on important part. The *sher* of Urdu is usually a couplet. The poet or *shair* reads the first line twice, sometimes thrice and then closes the idea in the second line wittily. Pope makes a plea for the heroic couplet as it is regular, symmetrical, witty and hence pleasing to the ear. In other words, it should be musical and harmonious, not cacophonous. He says:

Some beauties yet no precepts can declare,
For there's a happiness as well as care.
Music resembles poetry; in each
Are nameless graces which no methods teach
And which a master hand alone can reach. (140-44)

After this he says that deviations will lead to harshness. The events of nature like the sunrise, the sunset, the solar and lunar eclipses and the cycle of seasons are all regular and orderly. Any deviation in the occurrence of these natural phenomena is inconceivable. Likewise, poetry and music must follow the rules of order, symmetry and harmony. However, some deviations are permitted if they do not offend the basic rules. Deviations should promote the end.

In prospects, thus, some objects please our eyes,
Which out of nature's common order rise,
The shapeless rock, or hanging precipice
But though the ancients thus their rules invade,

(As kings dispense with laws themselves have made)
Moderns, beware! or if you must offend
Against the precept, never transgress its end. (158-64)

It follows then that deviations and experiments are allowed in poetry and art but they have to be within limits. For example, caesura in iambic pentameter is a regular feature and it should fall on the third foot but it may fall, occasionally, on the second foot. Similarly, metaphors are an integral part of poetry but a poet cannot mix too many things at a time. This is why John Drydén, Dr. Johnson and other critics denounced John Donne on the ground that he took mataphors from theology in his love poems like "Extasie" and "Airs and Angels".

Pope advises his fellowmen:

Let it be seldom, and compelled by need;
And have, at least, their precedent to plead.
The critic else proceeds without remorse,
Seizes your fame, and puts his laws in force. (165-68)

If young poets follow nature and her laws, they will be wits in the true sense of the term. They should not be presumptuous nor arrogant. Humility to ancients is of paramount importance. He greets the ancient bards who followed nature.

Hail, bards triumphant! born in happier days;
Immortal heirs of universal praise!
Whose honours with increase of ages grow,
As streams roll down, enlarging as they flow. (189-92)

II

Section II of the poem is concerned with the relationship between man and nature and the causes that make him unnatural. Griffin comments:

> The second section of the *Essay* (lines 203-559),...is devoted to "causes hindering a true judgement", and Pope presents most of these causes—pride, imperfect learning, judging by parts—as errors that can be avoided.[8]

The section begins with the first cause—pride—the cause that led Satan to fight with God and suffer eternal damnation. Man must be wary of this vice. If he is proud and not humble, his judgement shall be faulty and erroneous.

> Of all the causes which conspire to blind
> Man's erring judgement, and misguide the mind,
> What the weak head with strongest bias rules,
> Is pride, the never-failing vice of fools. (201-04)

After stating that pride is the basic vice of fools, Pope goes on to explain how ignorance and pride vitiate man's mind. A fool, because of his pride, tries to hide his ignorance. He makes a wrong judgement on something out of ignorance and when it is pointed out that he is in the wrong he asserts that his judgement is flawless. Pope continues to say that we should learn to be humble and listen to the wise people. If we do so, the truth will come to us in all its clarity.

> Pride, where wit fails, steps into our defence,
> And fills up all the mighty void of sense.
> If once right reason drives that cloud away,
> Truth breaks upon us with resistless day. (209-12)

The best thing for a person is to remain in doubt if things are not fully known, and try to know his own defects. Only then he will come to realise the truth that shines like the sun.

There is an old saying in Sanskrit that an ignorant can be taught and a scholar can be taught more easily but the person whose knowledge is shallow cannot be taught even by Brahma. The same thing is said by Pope in a different way:

> A little learning is a dangerous thing
> Drink deep or taste not the Pierian spring
> There shallow draughts intoxicate the brain,
> And drinking largely sobers us again. (215-18)

Pierian spring is the fountain of poetry. The word "drink" is applicable to both liquor and Pierian spring. When a person drinks a little wine he brags and raves but when he takes it full he becomes sober. So is the case with a critic. If he knows a little, he will talk a lot but after a deep study of poetry he will be sober and judicious. Here Pope lays down the general proposition that total ignorance is preferable to imperfect knowledge. The context shows that he is speaking of the conceited critics who are imperfect in their knowledge of literature. He tells these persons that the more enlightened they become the more judicious they will grow.

The next twenty lines compare the pursuit of knowledge with that of climbing the Alps. When a person starts climbing he sees the hill before him and feels it an easy task to reach the top. After reaching the top, he finds another taller hill. In this way he goes on climbing but every time he reaches the top he finds another mountain challenging him. Pope conveys this idea in his terse style:

So pleased at first the towering Alps we try,
Mount over the vales, and seem to tread the sky,
The eternal snow appear already past
And the first clouds and mountains seem the last:
But those attained, we tremble to survey
The growing labours of the lengthened way,
The increasing prospect tires our wandering eyes,
Hills peep over hills, and Alps on Alps arise! (227-34)

We, too, feel, after reading a little that we have gained and remain self-satisfied. But once we move on we find that knowledge is endless.

Fired at first sight with what the muse imparts
In fearless youth we tempt the height of arts
While from the bounded level of our mind
Short views we take, not see the lengths behind,
But more advanced, behold with strange surprise,
New distant scenes of endless science rise. (221-26)

Here Pope advises the critic to study deeply. It is only after wide reading that a critic gains knowledge. Besides, realizing the vastness of knowledge, he becomes humble. He says:

A perfect judge will read each work of wit
With the same spirit that its author writ:

Survey the whole, nor seek slight faults to find
Where nature moves and rapture warms the mind.
(235-38)

By introducing "nature" in line number 234 Pope lays emphasis on the wholeness of nature and art. Aristotle laid emphasis on the wholeness of art in *Poetics*. He said that a plot is a whole and its parts whole and together all the parts make a plot which is whole and beautiful. Pope also lays emphasis on the wholeness of art. A work of art or piece of poetry must not be judged by the beauty of a line nor be criticized if a line or two are faulty. It is the total impression which is to be counted.

In wit, as nature, what affects our hearts
Is not the exactness of peculiar parts;
'Tis not a lip, or eye, we beauty call
But the joint force and full result of all. (243-46)

He explains his point of view by referring to the famous dome of St. Peter's Cathedral in Rome.

Thus when we view some well-proportioned dome
(The world's just wonder, and even thine, O Rome!)
No single parts unequally surprise,
All comes united to the admiring eyes;
No monstrous height, or breadth, or length appear;
The whole at once is bold, and regular. (247-52)

A poem or a work of art should be judged keeping in view the author's or artist's intention and the means he has employed to achieve the end. He may deviate from the norms for the desired expression. But this deviation, if within limits, should not be criticised. It is the totality of a work of art which is of significance.

As men of breeding, sometimes men of wit,
To avoid great errors, must the less commit:
Neglect the rules each verbal critic lays
For not to know some trifles is a praise. (259-62)

What Pope says here, he himself has done in line 251 where the verb "appear" should have been singular, he has made it plural for a perfect rhyme with the word "regular" in line 252.

He regrets that some critics are so much interested in hair splitting that they do not see the woods for trees.

Most critics, fond of some subservient art,
Still make the whole depend upon a part;
They talk of principles, but notions prize,
And all to one loved folly sacrifice. (263-66)

He tells the story of a knight and a band. The band discussed poetry with the Knight and then produced their play before the knight and sought his comments on it. The Knight read it but was angry for the reason that there was no fight in the play. He failed to see that the subject, the plot, the manners, passions and unities were exactly according to rule. The remark that combat was left provoked the players and the leader commented angrily:

Not so, by heaven! he answers in a rage,
Knights, squires and steeds, must enter on the stage
So vast a throng the stage can never contain. (277-79)

Pope makes his observation and lays emphasis on the importance of the whole and casts aspersion on the critics who give undue importance to parts.

Thus critics of less judgement than caprice
Curious not knowing, not exact but nice,
Form short ideas; and offend in arts
As most in manners, but a love to parts. (285-88)

It is not proper to consider conceit as the only quality of poetry. Figures of speech and glittering lines are only ornaments; they are not nature. Poets of lesser quality being more concerned with ornamentation forget nature:

Poets like painters, thus unskilled to trace
The naked nature and the living grace
With gold and jewels cover every part,
And hide with ornaments their want of art. (293-96)

Wit is not the soul of poetry. Poetry must imitate nature. Here are the famous lines:

True wit is nature to advantage dressed
What oft was thought but never so well expressed.
(297-98)

After this, Pope comments on poetic diction and style. A true poet imitates nature faithfully and dresses the sublime thoughts in a sparkling diction. But if he is more interested in language and not in the sublimity of thought, his poetry becomes a luxuriant tree without fruit.

Abundance of words is a disqualification and, so it is always better to express great ideas in plain words. He says that verbosity is not a virtue of a poet; it is rather a defect.

Others for language all their care express
And value books, as women, men, for dress:
Their praise is still—the style is excellent;
The sense, they humbly take upon content.
Words are like leaves; and where they most abound,
Much fruit of beneath is rarely found. (310-15)

There must be a correlation between sense and sound. Mere sound is empty or it is what Shakespeare said through *Macbeth*:

It is a tale told by an idiot
Full of sound and fury, signifying nothing.

Pope remarks with a subtle irony:

A vile conceit in pompous words expressed
Is like a clown in regal purple dressed.

Therefore, he advises his fellowmen to make use of diction and metre judiciously and follow the examples of the great classical poets. According to him, iambic pentameter is the most majestic metre but its handling is really delicate. He tells us about the pitfalls:

These equal syllables alone require,
Tho' oft the ear the open vowels tire;
While expletives their feeble aid do join;
And ten low words oft creep in one dull line. (344-47)

Then again, there should be proper rhyme in a couplet. The rhyme should be meaningful also. Meaningless rhymes destroy the beauty of a heroic couplet. Similarly, a needless hexameter makes a line slow and awkward:

A needless alexandrine ends the song,
That, like a wounded snake, drags its slow length along.
(356-57)

Here Pope has deliberately used hexameter in the second line to illustrate how slow an alexandrine can be. Spenser ended his stanzas with alexandrines brilliantly but everybody cannot do so. What is important is the correlation between sound and sense.

'Tis not enough no harshness gives offence,
The sound must seem an echo to the sense. (364-65)

Poets and critics must not go to extremes. They should follow Aristotle's golden mean. This idea is in consonance with that of balance in nature.

Avoid extremes; and shun the fault of each,
Who still are pleased too little or too much
At every trifle scorn to take offence,
That always shows great pride, or little sense. (384-87)

The diction of a poem should correspond to its subject matter and emotion. The words should be soft and gentle while describing the spring season, be highly formal while making comments, ridicule should not be vulgar and must be tinged with subtle irony and while expressing wrath words should be hoarse and rough "like the torrent roar/ When Ajax strives some rock's vast weight to throw".

Pope's ideal is his predecessor John Dryden who wrote in different styles matching the subject matters and emotions. He praises Dryden's varied style:

Hear how Timotheus' varied lays surprise,
And bid alternate passions fall and rise!
While at each change, the son of Libyan Jove
Now burns with glory, and then melts with love;
Now his fierce eyes with sparkling fury glow,

Now sighs steal out, and tears begin to flow.
Persians and Greeks like turns of nature found,
And the world's victor stood subdued by sound!
The power of music all our hearts allow
And what Timotheus was, is Dryden now. (374-83)

Then he comes to the divergent views held by his contemporaries. One group favours the ancients but the other group the moderns. Pope says that we should not be involved in such disputes as to blame the ancients or praise them. Writers should be judged by their respective merits.

Regard not then if wit be old or new
But blame the false, and value still the true. (406-07)

He exhorts the critics to be balanced in their reasoning and be free from all kinds of prejudice. There are some critics who never hold their own views. They reason but conclude by predecents which are stale and almost rotten. Among the blind followers of the past popular but absurd views the worst are those who are ever ready to carry nonsensical ideas to their patrons. Generally, these people are always changing their opinions. Pope ridicules them.

Some praise at morning what they blame at night
But always think the last opinion right.
A muse by these is like a mistress used
This hour she's idolized, the next abused.
While their weak heads, like towns unfortified
'Twixt sense and nonsense daily change their sides.
(430-35)

These young people consider themselves wiser than the old people. Pope laughs at them with a wise saying.

We think our fathers fools, so wise we grow;
Our wiser sons, no doubt, will think us so. (438-39)

The most important task of a poet is to understand human nature and save it from all kinds of aberration. The great hindrance is that we praise those qualities in other men, which are present in us. This is a kind of egotism. We should be humble and appreciative of other people's qualities. Dryden was such a poet who was free from all kinds of malice and avarice and truthfully followed Homer. Homer was badly criticised by Zoilus and so was Dryden by Blackmore and Milbourne. But who cares for the invective of these critics? Their pride, malice and greed led them to their own defame. Dryden and Homer survived their criticism:

> Pride, malice, folly, against Dryden rose,
> In various shapes of persons, critics, beans;
> But sense survived when merry jests were past
> For rising merit will buoy up at last.
> Might he return, and bless once more our eyes,
> New Blackmores and new Milbournes must arise:
> Nay should great Homer lift his awful head,
> Zoilus again would start up from the dead. (458-65)

Pope says that their criticism proves the merit of Homer and Dryden.

> Envy will merit, as its shade, pursue;
> But like a shadow, proves the substance true. (466-67)

An unsubstantial thing cannot have a shadow; only substantial things have shadows. Likewise criticism is the shadow which proves the substance of a literary work. He illustrates his statement with a Homeric simile.

> For envied wit, like Sol eclipsed, makes known
> The opposing body's grossness, not its own
> When first that sun too powerful beams displays.
> It draws up vapours which obscure its rays
> But even those clouds at last adorn its way,
> Reflect new glories and augment the day. (468-73)

He is critical of his contemporaries who do not follow nature and disregard ancient writers like Homer, Virgil and Petrarch. He says that these moderns' works will not last a long time. They will die along with their authors. The greats are Chaucer and Dryden who followed the ancients. For him Dryden is a modern poet who has set an example before the writers of the eighteenth century:

Short is the date, alas! of modern rhymes,
And 'tis but just to let them live betimes,
No longer now that golden age appears,
When patriarch wits survived a thousand years:
Now length of fame (our second life) is lost,
And bare threescore is all even that can boast;
Our sons their fathers' failing language see,
And such as Chaucer is, shall Dryden be. (476-83)

After this he criticises his shallow contemporaries vehemently, those contemporaries who denounced Dryden and his followers. Pope says that these people boast of their poetry but it is worthless. It has no substance. It is as ephemeral as a flower. A flower lasts till it blooms. Soon it fades and its petals are strewn by the wind. These poet-critics, he says, will not be remembered after some time.

Unhappy wit, like most mistaken things,
Atones not for that envy which it brings,
In youth alone its empty praise we boast
But soon the short-lived vanity is lost. (494-97)

He exhorts his critics to shun their unnatural ways and follow the time-hallowed tradition founded by Homer, followed by the ancient Greeks and Romans and, in England, by Chaucer and Dryden. They should not try to seek praise by condemning the noble writers. And then he gives the wise advice which is always quoted by us:

Good nature and good sense must ever join
To err is human, to forgive, divine. (524-25)

This section ends with a reference to the titans who fought against gods and lost the war. It was presumptuous of them to wage a war against Zeus, the supreme god. Similary, the modern poets and critics must not be hostile to great writers. If they find fault with poets like Dryden, the defect lies not in the celebrated poet but in their own vision. The prejudiced critics find fault with everything good. Pope cites the example of the person who is suffering from jaundice:

All seems infected that the infected spy
As all looks yellow to the jaundiced eye. (558-59)

Section III is concerned with the poet-critic's morality, humility and propriety. The opening lines lay stress on morality:

Learn then what morals critics ought to show
For 'tis but half a judge's task, to know,
'Tis not enough, taste, judgement, learning, join,
In all you speak let truth and candour shine. (560-63)

What Pope lays stress on is truth and openness or what we say in our days transparency. Taste, judgement and knowledge are all important but they are all means to attain or know truth. Since truth is difficult to ken, it is important that the critic or poet should he cautious in any kind of pronouncement.

Be silent always when you doubt your sense;
And speak, though sure, with seeming difference.
(366-67)

However, the knowledge of truth is not sufficient. A person must speak truth in a pleasant way. A blunt statement will create many enemies.

'Tis not enough your counsel still be true;
Blunt truths more mischief than nice falsehood do;
Men must be taught as if you taught them not,
And things unknown proposed as things forgot
Without good breeding truth is disapproved. (578-82)

This advice of Pope compares favourably with the famous Sanskrit *shloka*:

Satyam bruyat priyam bruyat
Na Bruyat satyam apriyam
(Speak the truth but it should be pleasant, never state a truth which is unpleasant.)

When a person speaks pleasantly, we assume that he has been bred well. Secondly, one should not give advice without being asked. It is better that one should be sparing in giving advice. However, one should not shirk from giving advice or stating an unpleasant truth, if justice demands it. Thirdly, we should remain calm and quiet if the other party is a big fool. A wise person cannot compete with a person who does not understand things and goes railing at a good advice.

Your silence there is better than your spite,
For who can rail so long as they can write? (603-04)

Pope continues to say that there are many foolish poets and critics who, if given a good advice, will go beserk. They boast that they have read every writer and that they are omniscient. He writes sarcastically about them.

No place so sacred from such fops is barred
Nor is Paul's Church more safe than Paul's Churchyard
Nay, fly to altars there they'll talk you dead
For fools rush in where angels fear to tread. (622-25)

The last line of the quoted passage has become a classic quote. E.M. Forster gave the title *Where Angels Fear to Tread* to one of his novels. Besides, the line reveals Pope's great quality of saying wise things in the fewest words possible—what was oft thought but never so well-expressed.

The lines 630-42 describe the qualities of a good critic:

But where's the man, who counsel can bestow,
Still pleased to teach, and yet not proud to know?
Unbiased, or by favour, or by spite;
Not dully prepossessed, nor blindly right;
Though learn'd, well bred; and though well-bred sincere;
Modestly bold, and humanly severe.
Who to a friend his faults can freely show,
And gladly praise the merit of a foe?
Blest with a taste exact, yet unconfined;
A knowledge both of books and human kind;
Generous converse; a soul exempt from pride;
And love to praise with reason on his side?

After stating the qualities of the ideal critic-poet, Pope enumerates the critics whom he considers really great. The first are the critics of Greece and Rome in the classical age. The foremost critic, of course, is Aristotle who is called "the mighty Stagyrite" in the quoted passage. Since Aristotle was born in Stagira in Greece, he is called Stagyrite:

Such once were critics, such the happy few,
Athens and Rome in better ages knew.
The mighty Stagyrite first left the shore,
Spread all his sails, and durst the deeps explore;
He steered securely, and discovered far,
Led by the light of the Maeonian star. (644-49)

The next poet is Horace, the famous writer of *Ars Poetica* to whom Pope owes much. Besides, Horace was a poet par excellence and the kind of ode he wrote is called the Horatian ode.

Horace still charms with graceful negligence,
And without method talks us into sense;
Will like a friend, familiarly convey
The truest notion in the easiest way. (653-56)

We all know that Horace was essentially a poet and laid greater emphasis on decorum or propriety in poetry. Pope praised him for his aphoristic style and to a large extent followed him.

The next critic is Quintilian. We have forgotten him in our age but he was highly appreciated in the eighteenth century. Pope praises him:

In grave Quintilian's copious work, we find
The justest rules, and clearest method joined. (669-70)

The fourth classical critic is Longinus, author of *Peri Hupsos* or *On the Sublime*, who is read with great interest after Aristotle and Horace:

Thee, bold Longinus! all the Nine inspire
And bless their critic with a poet's fire
An ardent judge, who, zealous in his trust
With warmth gives sentence, yet is always just;
Whose own example strengthens all his laws;
And is himself that great sublime he draws. (675-80)

The minor critics followed the principles laid down by Aristotle, Horace, Quintilian and Longinus. The result was rewarding and both poetry and criticism flourished in the past.

> Thus long succeeding critics justly reigned,
> Licence repressed, and useful laws ordained.
> Learning and Rome alike in an empire grew;
> And arts still followed where her eagles flew. (681-84)

Later on, there was arrival of Christianity. The Christian morals were introduced. Erasmus was the first person who pleaded for the Christian morals.

> At length Erasmus, that great injured name,
> (The glory of the priesthood and the shame!)
> Stemmed the wild torent of a barbarous age,
> And drove those holy vandals off stage. (693-96)

The phrase "and the shame" in the second line has been explained by Crocker, one of the editors of Pope's works, as follows:

> The 'glory' from his own greatness, the "shame" from the rancour with which some of his brothers of priests assailed him.

It follows then that the word "shame" is not used against the eminent theologian; it is used for his critics who were priests. It was for Erasmus that poetry and art flourished in Rome and order, regularity and harmony prevailed everywhere:

> Rome's ancient genius, over its ruins spread,
> Shakes off the dust, and rears his reverend head.
> Then sculpture and her sister-arts revive;
> Stones leaped to form, and rocks began to live;
> With sweeter notes each rising temple rung
> A Raphael fainted and a Vida sung. (699-704)

But, after the passage of time, poetry moved to France:

> Thence arts over all the northern world advance,
> But critic-learning flourished most in France
> The rules a nation, born to serve, obeys;
> And Boilean still in right of Horace sways. (711-14)

Finally, Pope pays tribute to Roscommon whom he calls "Nature's Chief Master-piece". His real name was Wentworth Dillon and he was the fourth Earl of Roscommon (1633-85). He wrote *Essay on Translated Verse* (1684) and made a blank verse translation of Horace's *Ars Poetica* in 1680 and titled it *The Art of Poetry*. He was among the first to recognise the greatness of Milton's *Paradise Lost*.

Because of his classical bent, he is praised by Pope:

> Such was Roscommon, not more learned than good
> With manners generous as his noble blood;
> To him the wit of Greece and Rome was known,
> And every author's merit, but his own. (725-28)

Along with him is counted William Walsh (1663-1708), Dryden's contemporary who encouraged young Pope by praising the *Pastorals* (*Eclogues*), analysed in the second chapter of this book and suggesting improvements to them. The poem ends with the advice:

> Content, if hence the unlearned their wants may view,
> The learned reflect on what before they knew:
> Careless of censure, nor too fond of fame;
> Still pleased to praise, yet not afraid to blame,
> Averse alike to flatter, or offend
> Not free from faults, nor yet too vain to mend.
> (709-14)

In short, a true poet-critic should maintain equanimity in all situations.

Essay on Criticism, though revised at a later stage, is the work of a brilliant young poet. Pope's achievement lies in the fact that he has summarised the basic principles of literary criticism, not by explication but by practical implication. The first section, following Aristotle's model, describes the concept of the universe as envisaged by scientists and philosophers of the renaissance period and understood by the eighteenth century intellectuals. The basic idea is that God is creater of the universe and nature is His art and if poets and critics follow nature, they imitate God's art. Imitation was not supposed to be something base in Pope's time. On the other hand, it was the duty of the poet to imitate the greats. Pope himself did it. He told his friend Spence:

> My first taking to imitating was not out of vanity but humility: I saw how defective my own things were; and endeavoured to mend my manner, by copying good strokes from others.

Quoting this passage Rebecca Price Parkin comments:

> Humility, aside from being good and common sense, was part of the public decorum of a young poet. The Augustan audience expected the young poet to defer to tradition to measure himself against it, and to be always aware how unlikely it was that everybody was out of step but Joe. Pope voices his consciousness of this attitude in, among other places, *Essay on Criticism*.[9]

In fact, *Essay on Criticism* is a manual on how to write good poetry and be its good judge. The first section advises young writers to follow nature. They can do so by following the great classical poets. To be a good judge, a person must be humble, studious and free from all kinds of prejudice. The second section lays stress on humility, righteousness and deep knowledge.

The last section counts the names of the great critics who observed order, regularity and harmony in nature and the English critic the Earl of Roscommon, popularly called Roscommon because:

> To him the wit of Greece and Rome was known
> And every author's merit, but his own. (717-18)

We read *Essay on Criticism* not only for its being an ancient work of literary criticism and representing the basic principles of writing poetry in the eighteenth century but also for its sparkling wit and wise sayings.

Notes

1. *Works of Alexander Pope*, p. 37. All quotations from *Essay on Criticism* are from the *Works*. From here onwards only line numbers are given in parentheses at the end of the quoted passages.
2. W.K. Wimsatt and Cleanth Brooks, *Literary Criticism: A Short History*, (Delhi: Oxford Book Company, 1957), p. 237.

3. Martin C. Battestin, *Providence of Wit*, pp. 1-2.
4. Bonamy Dobreé, *Oxford History of English Literature: The Early Eighteenth Century*, p. 190.
5. Dustin H. Griffin, *Alexander Pope: The Poet in the Poems*, pp. 83-84.
6. Ripley Hotch, *Pope Surveys His Kingdom: An Essay on Criticism*, *Studies in English Literature*, 13 (1973), pp. 474-87.
7. *Works*, Footnote, p. 39.
8. Dustin H. Griffin, *op. cit.*, p. 85.
9. R.P. Parkin, *The Poetic Workmanship of Pope* (Mineapolis: University of Minnesota Press, 1955), p. 184.

4

An Essay on Man

An Essay on Man is an ambitious poem written during the maturity period of Pope. It is more a philosophy than a poem, though its poetic quality is par excellence. It is surprising that the critics of his time did not consider it a good poem. Joseph Warton, one of the leading critics of the eighteenth century commented:

> *An Essay on Man* was a work of great labour and long consideration, but certainly not the happiest of Pope's performances. The subject is perhaps not very proper for poetry, and the poet was not sufficiently master of his subject.[1]

Now we know better. Professor G. Wilson Knight considers it a serious poem and great achievement of Pope:

> It is not only a poetic philosophy, but the universal philosophy, not so much of poets as of poetry; and is, exactly, the philosophy implied by Shakespeare's work.[2]

This poem is certainly a great achievement of Pope. He has stated his philosophy in the most poetic language. His greatness lies in the fact that he has been able to state profound philosophical ideas in poetry, sparkling with wit. The poem was published in parts in the years 1733-34. In 1735, Pope inserted the Four Epistles of *An Essay on Man* in his works and prefaced with "The Design". Let us remember that he, like Milton, has written "Argument" to each Epistle.

"The Design" which is Preface of the poem gives the idea of the poem's plan and the poet's own intention to express his philosophy of life through it. I quote the significant lines from "The Design". By "significant lines" I mean the lines which I feel to be significant.

"Having proposed to write some pieces on human life and manners such as to use my Lord Bacon's expression, come home to men's business and bosoms, I thought it more satisfactory to begin with considering man in the abstract, his nature and his state....

The science of human nature is, like all other sciences, reduced to a few clear points. There are not many certain truths in this world. It is, therefore, in the anatomy of the mind as in that of the body, more good will accrue to mankind by attending to the large, open and perceptible parts, than by studying too much such finer nerves and vessels, the conformations and uses of which will for ever escape our observation....

That I might have done in prose; but I chose verse, and even rhyme, for two reasons. The one will appear obvious, that principles, maxims, or precepts so written, both strike the reader more strongly at first, and are more easily retained by him afterwards. The other may seem odd, but is true. I found I could express them more shortly this way than in prose itself...."

Pope makes it clear that *An Essay on Man* is an essay in verse. In simple words, he has put in his idea of God, Universe, Man and Art in a long poem, not in a treatise in prose.

The poem consists of four Epistles with the following titles:

(i) "Of the Nature and State of Man with Respect to the Universe".

(ii) "Of the Nature and State of Man with Respect to Himself, as an Individual".

(iii) "Of the Nature and State of Man with Respect to Society".

(iv) "Of the Nature and State of Man with Respect to Happiness".

William Warburton, editor and commentator, was the first person to point out Pope's indebtedness to Viscount Henry St. John Bolingbroke. He wrote in the Introduction to *An Essay on Man*:

> *The Essay on Man* was at first given, as Mr. Pope told me, to Dr. Young, to Dr. Dasaguliers, to Lord Bolingbroke, to Lord Paget, and in short to everybody but to him who was capable of writing it. While several of his acquaintanus read *The Essay on Man* as the work of an unknown author, they fairly owned they did not understand it....
>
> The fact is that Bolingbroke was a radical in thought and a disgrace in politics and because of these, he had to leave England and stay in France in exile. Since Pope incorporated his idea of Deism to some extent and refuted Milton's popular assertion of justifying God's ways to man, he did not have the courage to publish the poem with his name printed as poet. It is only when the poem gained popularity, that he disclosed his name.[3]

Pope represents the rationality of the age and is more humble. He is scientific in the modern sense. He is concerned with man's place in the universe, the relationship between the individual and society and finally individual's quest for happiness.

The first Epistle has the following outline, called The Argument on the pattern of John Milton's *Paradise Lost*. The first two sentences are quoted here:

> Of man in the abstract—I. That we can judge only with regard to our own system, being ignorant of the relation of systems and things.... II. That man is not to be deemed imperfect, but a being suited to his place and rank in the creation, agreeable to the general order of things, and conformable to ends and relations to him unknown.[4]

He ends the Argument with the conclusion that pride, avarice and unreasonable desire are the prime causes of man's misery. It is necessary to submit oneself to Providence.

Epistle I: According to some critics, especially Maynard Mack and Pat Rogers, Epistles I and IV are the most impressive and very much relevant even today. As said earlier Viscount St. John Henry Bolingbroke is the inspiring force of the poem. Pope rightly addresses him in the opening lines:

> Awake, my St. John! leave all meaner things
> To low ambition, and the pride of Kings.
> Let us (since life can little more supply
> Than just to look about us, and to die,)
> Expatiate free over all this scene of man. (I, 1-5)

The use of the possessive "my" indicates Pope's affection for his friend. As Bolingbroke is the philosopher to guide Pope to Philosophy, Pope addresses him lovingly. We can also say that Pope is addressing his other self which is in hibernation. He asks the addressee to give up thinking about smaller and lighter things and meditate on serious philosophical concepts; man is not born to live and die for bread alone.

Just after the preliminaries, Pope comes to the main theme.

This world is:

> A mighty maze! but not without a plan;
> A wild, where weeds and flowers promiscuous shoot;
> Or garden, tempting with forbidden fruit.
> Together let us beat this ample field
> Try what the open, what the covert yield;
> The latent tracts, the giddy heights explore
> Of all who blindly creep, or sightless soar;
> Eye nature's walks, shoot folly as it flies,
> And catch the manners living as they rise
> Laugh where we must, be candid where we can;
> But vindicate the ways of God to man. (I, 6-16)

The fourth line in the quoted passage: "Together let us beat this ample field"—is an indicator of the collaboration of ideas between Pope and Bolingbroke and the last line takes us back to Milton and *Paradise Lost.* Milton's aim in *Paradise Lost* was to justify the ways of God to man; why man ate the fruit of the forbidden tree and why he was sent to the earth. His point of view is religious. Here Pope under the influence of Bolingbroke surveys the universe and God's plan and vindicates His plan why He made such a plan for man.

This universe is a large labyrinth which seems rather haphazard and confusing but in fact it has been created according to a plan. The question the poet puts is whether it is a forest where weeds and flowers grow promiscuously or it is a garden where all are at their right place. In order to know the design, it is advisable to go through it and trace out the plan. There are varieties and contrasts—deeps and heights, fields and forests.

Dustin H. Griffin's explanation of the quoted passage is worth quoting here. I quote the sentences which, I think are more important:

> The opening paragraph, addressed to Bolingbroke, expresses above all Pope's sense of his own adequacy to his task. He exudes the casual confidence of the gentleman philosopher who can 'expatiate' as easily over 'the scene of man' as he can wander.... The business is a worthy way to spend one's time (better than politics) but nothing to be solemn or strenuous about.... Though his time is but 'a moment' and his space but 'a point', he fully dominates that span of life....
>
> The audacity, underlined by Pope's allusion to Milton, is surely intended.... It implies a kind of teasing distinction between man's concern and God's, man's work and God's. Whatever else it does, 'but' prevents the final line from being the paragraph's rhetorical climax, the end points towards which everything moves. By contrast, Milton's grand paragraph expands phrase by pulsing phrase in a single sentence building tension as it swells, until all is resolved in the final declaration: 'I may assert Eternal Providence/ And justify the ways of God to men.' By contrast, Pope first establishes his own worldly identity quite apart from God, and he emphatically sets God at a distance....
>
> The comparison with the opening lines of *Paradise Lost* might be extended to remark that Bolingbroke corresponds

> to Milton's 'Heavenly Muse'; both are directly addressed, both bid to 'say first'. But where Milton humbly petitions his all-powerful muse for instruction and light.... Pope clearly sets himself on a part with 'my St. John'. Where Milton's prayer gives all the credit to the muse who will alone make it possible for him to succeed, Pope's 'Vindicate' lies clearly within his and Bolingbroke's own power.[5]

If we follow Griffin's interpretation (he has quoted profusely from Pope's letters to Swift and also William Empson's interpretation in *Seven Types of Ambiguity*), we arrive at the conclusion that Pope's aim is modest, a middle flight in comparison to Milton's comprehensive and high flight. He wants to "laugh where we must, be candid where we can". In other words, his aim is to make mankind look upon life with comfort and pleasure and put morality in good order.

Pope continues the Epistle in the manner of Milton:

> Say first, of God above, or man below,
> What can we reason, but from
> Of man, what see we but his station here,
> From which to reason, or to which refer?
> Thro' worlds unnumbered tho' God be known
> 'Tis ours to trace Him only in our own. (I, 17-22)

Here Pope's aim is more clear. Milton is concerned with God's purpose in allowing Satan to misguide man; Pope, because by his time science had advanced a lot, wanted to read God's design of the universe and man's place in this world. In short, Milton's approach is religious whereas Pope's is social; Milton is concerned with the race of man against evil but Pope is concerned with man in society. However, he never ignores God, universe and nature.

As already mentioned in the first chapter Pope is more concerned with the system of nature and the vast design of God. These lines describe the system of the universe as it was interpreted in the eighteenth century. It is important to note that Copernicus, Galileo, Newton and Leibnitz were established figures in Pope's time and there was no need to refute them or even defend them. Pope's stress is on reason:

> See worlds on worlds compose one universe,
> Observe how system into system runs
> What other planets circle other suns
> What varied being peoples every star
> May tell why Heaven has made us as we are!
>
> (I, 24-28)

Pope accepts the scientific truth that the sun is a star and there are many stars like the sun in this universe, that each star has several planets and that they are all varied and different from our earth. All planets and stars move under a system which is quite complex.

In the next paragraph, Bolingbroke is absent. The addressee is the reader. Pope stands at a higher pedestal. He asks people to be humble and benign as he is feeble and weak, an insignificant part of the universe.

> Is the great chain, that draws all to agree,
> And drawn supports, upheld by God or thee?
> Presumptuous man! the reason wouldst thou find,
> Why formed so weak, so little and so blind? (I, 33-36)

Pope says that everything is made under the system. The child may ask its mother why the oak is so large and strong and the weeds are so small and weak. There is reason behind the variety and contrast in our world and that is God's reason which is followed by nature.

> Of systems possible, if 'tis confest
> That wisdom infinite must form the best,
> Where all must-full or coherent be,
> And all that rises, rise in due degree. (I, 43-46)

When everything grows and attains perfection in due course, it is plain that man by virtue of his superior wisdom has got a superior and distinct place in this universe. Now the problem is what kind of relationship man shall have with the universe. In other words, what his actions should be. With regard to his actions we cannot say which are absolutely good or absolutely bad. Fate is not everything. There is the freewill. Man must struggle to achieve the desired goals. But he must not question the Divine Order, although he is the perfect creature created by God.

> Then say not man's imperfect, Heaven's in fault;
> Say rather, man's as perfect as he ought.
> His knowledge measured to his state and place,
> His time a moment, and a point his space. (I, 69-72)

The book of fate is hidden from the sight of man. Pope gives examples from the lives of the horse and the ox. Man rides the horse fast. The ox also works for man in the field. The ox breaks the earth with its hooves. But at other times it is overpowered by other animals. Next time, it is chosen by the Egyptian who deify it and worship it for twenty-five years. Neither the horse nor the bull is able to understand why there are so many changes in the fortune of their lives. God's ways are mysterious. Man, like the ox and the bull or any other creature on the earth, cannot understand why so many changes come into his life. Here, Pope follows the message of God in the *Book of Job*. Job, a pious man, prospers but later on suffers immeasurably. He questions God. God's reply comes through a whirlwind. He asks Job to look at things around him and see His power. God watches everything and His ways are inscrutable.[6]

The idea expressed in *Book of Job* is stated in a slightly different way. We must not ask questions about God's justice or His Plan; He is merciful to all.

> Oh blindness to the future! kindly given,
> That each may fill the circle marked by Heaven:
> Who sees with equal eye, as God of all,
> A hero perish, or a sparrow fall,
> Atoms or systems into ruin hurled
> And now a bubble burst, and now a world. (I, 85-90)

Therefore, man should remain hopeful always, even amidst adversity. But he must not be arrogant. He should adore God because nobody knows what gift He would give him in future:

What future bliss, he gives not thee to know,
But gives that hope to be thy blessing now.
Hope springs eternal in the human breast. (I, 93-95)

Pope cites the example of the Indian people. It is very difficult to say what Indian he refers to. The Indian may be from the USA (the Red Indian), or from the West Indies (West Indian). His peaceful, innocent and honest life is described in lines 100-12. They are paraphrased here:

Look at the Indian. He is innocent and free from any kind of questioning. He sees God in clouds or hears him in the sound of the wind. As he is ignorant, his soul never would expect to reach the Milky Way where all noble souls go after death. Yet his simple and naive nature has given him a simple faith. He believes that Heaven is somewhere behind the hills capped with snow. His belief is that there is a world of comfort in the depth of the forest. There is an island of joy in the middle of the ocean. There they enjoy and rest without cruel treatment from their wicked masters. That land is not inhabited by the money-minded Christians. He is content with simple things; he does not hope for miracles in life. He does not expect the patronage of an angel nor does he think that a seraph will ever come to him holding a burning coal with tongs to purge him of his iniquity and sins. His ambition is rather low. He feels he will be happy because he will live under the sky with his masters or owners and his faithful dog will keep company with him.

Here, Pope's humanity is easily traceable. In those days, black people from the West Indies and Red Indians of America were caught and sold in the market by the white people. Their life was wretched. They suffered miserably but did not know the main cause of suffering. Here Pope hits the white people, the money-minded Christians.

He exhorts his fellowmen to follow the path of humility. It will be a folly if they consider themselves wise and find fault with God's justice and ways. If they say that God destroys all His creatures for mere sport or that He has been unjust to them by depriving them of their happiness, they can do so. But will they, by doing so, break themselves away from the hand of God, take His sceptre and become God themselves? This rhetorical question is an answer in itself.

Pride is the greatest sin and humility is the greatest virtue:

In pride, in reasoning pride, our error lies;
All quit their sphere, and rust into the skies. (I, 123-24)

Pope elaborates the idea in subsequent lines. If pride is there in man he will always look high into the sky and aspire to be angels. When angels are proud they will try to be gods. But if they aspire to be gods, they will fall and similarly men, aspiring to be angels, will fall. There are the divine laws and any person, who wants to invert the laws of order, will commit sin against God.

The whole universe is an order and it runs at the will of God but a proud man will say that all that is happening is meant for him. He will say that stars shine for him, the earth is for him, the herbs, the flowers, honey and all the treasures belong to him. But this is his presumptuousness.

We should remember that all the phenomena of nature are the parts of God's system. They are independent of man's wishes. Natural events like earthquake, tempest and big flood occur not because man wants them but because they are the result of God's eternal laws.

...the first almighty cause
Acts not by partial, but by general laws;
The exceptions few.... (I, 145-47)

After stating that God is not for a few and nature is for all, he comes to man and happiness.

If the great end be human happiness
Then nature deviates; and can man do less?
As much that end a constant course requires
Of showers and sun-shine, as of human desire.
As much eternal springs and cloudless skies,
As men for ever temperate, calm and wise. (I, 149-54)

Here Pope means to say that nature is created by God and so is man. Nature will function in its own and not for the pleasure or happiness of man. Man's life is full of ups and downs.

There are cloudy days and sunny days. He has to toil hard for happiness and try to become temperate, calm and wise. If things go against him, he should not accuse God. Caesar Borgia, the son of Pope Alexander VI or Sergius Catiline, the wicked Roman conspirator and traitor brought calamities to their people by their acts. Similarly, Julius Caesar and Alexander brought ruin to many countries by conquering them. We accuse them of harming mankind but we cannot blame God for their actions. We must not be that proud. The best thing for us is to submit to the Will of God in all humility.

Happiness or joy for man does not consist in thinking beyond his limit. He should not try to acquire for himself those things which his body and soul cannot hold or contain. He should mark the contrast between different kinds of insects and animals. The creatures that live in grass and bushes have keen eyes but the mole has dull eyes. The African lioness tries to locate her prey on hearing sounds but the hunting dogs depend on their power of smell.

Man is different from all the creatures of the world because animals and insects have the five senses of perception but man has reason or thought, in addition. This is because he can think he is the lord of all the creatures on the earth.

There is a hierarchy in this world. At the base is the inanimate matter in the ocean, in the air and on the earth which bursts into life. Then there are the insects and small creatures and then the big animals. The lower cannot take the place of the higher. This is order. If men were to press on powers superior to him, he should remember, powers inferior to him may as well press on him. The whole of this nature is bound together in a close linked chain and if one unit in this graded system of creation is broken, there will be anarchy and disorder. If each system connected so closely with the other tries to be independent of the control of the whole, there will be a complete breakdown.

Therefore, man should not try to break the order of things and follow the system of nature.

> The bliss of man (could pride that blessing find)
> Is not to act or think beyond mankind;

No powers of body, or of soul to share,
But what his nature and his state can bear. (I, 189-92)

He should look at the vast chain of being, which began from God and has come upto the microbes which the naked eye cannot see. His duty is to marvell at the wonder of creation. He must realize the truth that:

All are but parts of one stupendous whole,
Whose body nature is, and God the soul,
That changed through all, and yet in all the same
Great in the earth, as in the ethereal frame. (I, 267-70)

There is diversity and variety in God's creation. Nature is God's art. All things are counter and original. Man's happiness lies in surrendering to God in all humility and giving up all his pride.

All nature is but art unknown to thee;
All chance, direction which thou canst not see;
All discord, harmony not understood;
All partial evil, universal good;
And, spite of pride, in erring reason's spite
One truth is clear, 'Whatever is, is right'. (I, 289-94)

Epistle II is subtitled "Of the Nature and State of Man in Respect to Himself as an Individual". It follows the premises of the first Epistle. Man cannot interfere in the laws of God and thereby nature; he has to follow both. He is superior to animals only because God has made him so. There are two main principles that drive him forward in life. They are self-love and reason. Self-love is stronger than reason and it is the cause of all actions. Reason is the restraining power. It is the balancing and guiding principle.

This Epistle has one of the most quoted lines in its opening:

Know then thyself, presume not God to scan,
The proper study of mankind is man. (II, 1-2)

The influence of the renaissance is quite obvious here. It was during the renaissance that men of letters shifted their focus from the supernatural to the human. Renaissance heralded the beginning of humanism. The eighteenth century revived the Greek and Latin classicism more accurately. Aristotle's *golden mean* was accepted with a great fervour. Aristotle said that bravery is the golden mean of the extremes of cowardice and rashness. The idea that man should tread the middle path and that there should be a happy compromise between heart and mind is stated in the first paragraph of Epistle II. Man is in the middle of God and animals. Pope also follows Donne's words "All philosophy calls in doubt". Perhaps, he is influenced by Descartes who said, "I doubt, so I exist". His friend Bolingbroke propounded the same idea. Man is:

> A being darkly wise, and rudely great:
> With too much knowledge for the sceptic side
> With too much weakness for the stoic's pride
> He hangs between; in doubt to act, or rest;
> In doubt to deem him a god, or beast. (II, 3-7)

Man, according to Pope, is a bundle of contradictions, if he boasts to be perfect, he is in the wrong. In fact, he is always diffident and in doubt. He must not be proud of his status on the earth. He must not be too ambitious and arrogant. If he thinks that he can do everything, he should travel round the earth and map it or direct the planets to move in some other way. He should study Plato's writings thoroughly and rise above this earth to a region which is above all these sets of spheres in the sky.

Pope knows that man cannot do these things. So he advises him to imitate the ways of God. He should follow knowledge modestly, and without pride. Generally, people become proud after gaining knowledge. Pride must be discarded altogether, and also, showiness, idleness and all luxury of the body and mind that knowledge leads to. Let us be altogether free from the tendency that every man of knowledge has of showing some tricks of the brain merely for the sake of pleasure.

There are two main principles in human nature. The first is the love for one's own self. This compels a man to action. This impulse of self-love cannot be called entirely good or bad. If it is rightly applied, it is good and, if improperly or wrongly applied it is bad. Self-love is the source of all human activity and it must be controlled by reason which is the second principle. Reason compares one thing with another and distinguishes good from bad. Thus, both are complementary to each other. However, reason has the upper hand.

Passions, like elements, tho' born to fight
Yet, mixt and softened in his work unite;
Suffice that reason keep to nature's road
Subject, compound them, follow her and God.
Love, hope, and joy, fair pleasure's smiling train,
Hate, fear, and grief, the family of pain.
These mixt with art, and to due bounds confined
Make and maintain the balance of mind.
The lights and shades, whose well accorded strife
Gives all the strength and colour of our life.
(II, 113-22)

But reason cannot go against nature. All who are born are to die some day. People grow and in course of time become old. There is in the beginning the perfect balance of humours but later on any one of the four humours begins to dominate; diseases then come to them. In order that the body should be in sound health, there is the need to apply reason. Reason functions as a guard:

Yes, nature's road must ever be preferred;
Reason is here no guide, but still a guard. (II, 161-62)

In the competition between passion or self-love and reason, the latter must have the upper hand. Passion, though the main force of action, is rather blind. It can take man to the extremes. Man must follow the middle path. For this, he must act according to reason.

Extremes in nature equal ends produce
In man they join to some mysterious use;
Though each by turns the other's bound invade,
As, in some well-wrought picture, light and shade.
(II, 205-08)

As man is a mixture of both, reason can be his only guide. Man should never go to any extremes. If he considers himself perfectly virtuous, he is in the wrong. He is a mixture of both:

> Virtuous and vicious every man must be,
> Few in the extremes, but all in the degree. (II, 231-32)

Commenting on Pope's views as expressed in Epistle II, G. Wilson Knight writes:

> In Epistle II Pope concentrates on man. He attacks science, contrasting its supposed certitudes concerning the majestic and mysterious universe with man's hopeless ignorance of, and lack of mastery over himself. It then concentrates on the instinct of self-love as the primary thrust of human nature. Reason, we are told, can look ahead and guide, but is not the motor force. Pope sternly reproves thinkers who regard instinct and reason as enemies: "More studious to divide than to unite", they are happiest when "at war about a name:, and we may say the same about certain critical concepts that have since helped to fog the naturalistic synthesis of Pope's own *Essay*....
>
> All passions can be directed for good, they are indeed the necessary gale to drive on the ship; various emotions may be harmoniously blended; man cannot, we are told, destroy what he is himself composed of. We are urged towards a light-and-shade harmony tuned, with reason's help, to natural and divine purpose.[7]

That Pope's emphasis is more on man's frailty is the conclusion of Dustin's analysis of Epistle II. He writes:

> His basic theme, here as throughout the *Essay* is the providential order underlying apparent disorder.... What is remarkable, however, is how darkly Pope treats the commonplaces about man's divided nature, how much emphasis he places on man's limited comprehension, his self-delusion, his 'folly'.... Man's 'middle state' is of course an ancient topic of moral philosophers, a way of defining man's special place in the creation, his special powers and capacities, 'higher than the beasts but lower than the

angels', But Pope gives more emphasis to 'Frailties' and 'Limits' than to 'Powers'.[8]

We see the two critics clash. G. Wilson Knight is of the view that Pope's emphasis is on harmony but Dustin says that unconsciously Pope lays more emphasis on man's frailty. As my analysis has shown I am with G. Wilson Knight. However, the conclusion of the Epistle is forced. Pope has failed to arrive at a natural conclusion. Perhaps, his own deformity and frailty forbade him to reach the desired conclusion in Epistle II.

Epistle III is about the nature and state of man with respect to society. Nature is governed by divine laws and man by the laws of nature. His happiness lies in following nature. In Epistle II Pope says that man is pulled by the two extremes of goodness and badness. He is neither a beast nor an angel; he is a mixture of both. His self-love is the driving force of all actions. Reason is the guard. Once, he realizes this truth, he can gain happiness.

But man cannot live in isolation. After all he is a member of the human society. Pope gives his views on man's place in society. Following the previous arguments he says that man has to follow the same divine laws as described in the previous Epistles. Epistle III opens thus:

Here then wc rcst; The Universal Cause
Acts to one end, but acts by various laws.
In all the madness of superfluous health,
The trim of pride, the impudence of wealth,
Let this great truth be present night and day. (III, 1-5)

It may be pertinently asked what "this great truth" is. Pope explains "this great truth" in the second paragraph that it is "the great chain of love" which combines everything in this world. Atoms are in combination. Dying vegetation sustains the springing vegetation. All things in this world spring like bubbles that burst and mingle with the ocean. All objects of the world are controlled by the great chain of being.

Nothing is foreign; parts relate to whole;
One all-extending, all-preserving soul

Connects each being, greatest with the least;
Made beast in aid of man, and man of beast;
All served, all serving: nothing stands alone;
The chain holds on, and where it ends, unknown.
(III, 21-26)

What Pope has said in Epistle II, he repeats in the third paragraph that all the things created in this universe are not meant for man. Man like them is also a created being. Therefore, he should not feel proud. Birds and beasts do not obey man's call; they all obey God. He says ironically:

Know, nature's children all divide her care;
The fur that warms a monarch, warmed a bear.
(III, 43-44)

It may be said that the strong still control the weak. But man is not an animal. He has reason and wisdom. Besides, nature controls him gently by endowing him with mercy. He realizes the sufferings of others, men and animals both. The hawk that kills a bird or the jay bird that eats insects has no mercy. It is their nature to kill and eat. They cannot enjoy the beautiful song of a nightingale. It is man's nature to care for all. He has left the wood to the birds to fly freely about. Pastures are left for domestic animals and fish are allowed to swim in lakes and ponds. Man loves freedom and allows other creatures to enjoy freedom.

But there is a lacuna. He protects animals and birds from the predators, fattens them by feeding but, later on, kills and eats them. What is ironical is that he does realize the truth that he himself shall be killed by Death.

That very life his learned hunger craves,
He saves from famine, from the savage saves;
Nay feasts the animal he dooms his feast
And, till he ends the being, makes it blest;
Which sees no more the stroke, or feels the pain,
Than favoured man by touch ethereal slain.
The creature had his feast of life before;
Thou too must perish why thy feast is o'er. (III, 63-70)

God acts as friend to all those who are not gifted with reason. He does not allow man to have any knowledge of his end. He gives this much of knowledge to man that he will die some day but keeps him in dark about the time or moment of death. This also serves man at all times to gain happiness by quick nature. Heavier reason also works hard to gain this happiness. Human wit serves man at all times but reason does not stay long. God gives particular blessings to particular organisms according to their need. He has created an order in which mutual happiness depends on mutual wants and their satisfaction. Animals are joined to animals and men to men. Love is the binding force. All animals help one another and so do men. Every species runs on family system. Animals love their children and protect them from predators. Even the predators have family life. Love is the main reason for the continuance of the existent species on the earth.

There is a difference between man and other creatures. His children depend on their parents for a very long time. It is this longer care on the part of the parents that forms a more lasting connection between parents and children. Thoughtfulness and reason improve upon the relationship between the child and the parents.

It will bc wrong to think that man walked blindly into the state of nature. The state of nature was just the same as the kingdom of God. As creation came into existence, self-love and love of society grew in men. They unified all men into an organization. There was no pride then. Men, at that time, were not civilized in the modern sense. But there was no selfishness also. They lived in forests peacefully. But later on, violent passion made them fiercer and warmongering. Life changed from naivete to artificiality. Nature advised men to learn from animals and other creatures the art of living, how socially they live, the ants especially. Though the queen reigns over them, the ants and the bees live in order and harmony. There is no quarrel, no fighting. They all work in unison. Now nature advises men,

> Yet go! and thus o'er all the creatures sway
> Thus let the wiser make the rest obey;

And for those arts mere instinct could afford,
Be crowned as monarchs, or as gods adored.

(III, 195-98)

In the beginning man listened to nature's words and followed her faithfully. The result was:

Cities were built, societies were made:
Here rose one little state; another near
Grew by like means, and joined thro' love or fear.

(III, 200-02)

After the formation of the cities and societies came states and kings. The basis of the formation of states was love and liberty. Earlier the name of the king was unknown. Now, he became the head of the society or state and people obeyed him as sons and daughters obey their father. It was a happy growth of civilization as people obeyed nature.

Till then, by nature crowned, each patriarch state,
King, priest, and parent, of his growing state;
On him, their second Providence, they hung
Their law his eye, their oracle his tongue.

Every state was like an island, happy and peaceful under the governance of its king.

Man like his Maker, saw that all was right;
To virtue, in the paths of pleasure trod
And own'd a father when he own'd a God.

(III, 232-34)

Further,

True faith, true policy, united ran,
That was but love of God, and this of man

(III, 239-40)

But things have changed now. The poet asks in the manner of Milton in *Paradise Lost*.

Who first taught souls enslaved and realms undone
The enormous faith of many made for one;

That proud exception to all nature's laws
To invert the world, and counter-work its cause?
(III, 241-44)

In *Paradise Lost,* it is Satan who is responsible for man's fall from Paradise; here it is self-love. Describing the havoc brought by man's love for power and pleasure, Pope says:

So drives self love, thro' just and thro' unjust,
To one man's power, ambition, lucre, lust
The same self-love, in all, becomes the cause
Of what restrains him, government and laws.
(III, 269-72)

Finally,

Self-love forsook the path it first pursued,
And found the private in public good. (III, 281-82)

The condition became almost chaotic. The whole society was disintegrated. At that time philosophers, broad-minded intellectuals, religious and social leaders, poets and true patriots united together and raised their voice to restore the faith and moral values that mankind had lost. The old order as given by God was revived. As a result of this awakening God's shadow at least, if not His image, came down on the earth. Men and kings learnt now the correct use of self-love. They learnt not to be too slack nor to be too restrained. Pope uses a metaphor from music to describe the nature of order and harmony in human society.

Taught nor to slack, nor strain its tender strings,
The less, or greater, set so justly true
That touching one must strike the other too;
Till jarring interests of themselves create
Th' according music of a well-mixt state
Such is the world's great harmony, that springs
From order, union, full consent of things. (III, 290-96)

His final statement on the form of government is one of the most quoted lines:

For forms of government let fools contest
Whatever is best administered is best. (III, 303-04)

These lines if quoted out of context appear cynical. But, when considered in their context, they give us a profound truth. Pope is not concerned whether a democratic, aristocratic or monarchic government is better. He wants a society where all human beings maintain a balance between self-love and reason, where everybody, whether the king or the plebian, is in perfect harmony and follows nature and thereby the divine laws. He ends the third Epistle with the following lines:

> So two consistent motions act the soul:
> And one regards itself, and one the whole.
> Thus God and nature linked the general frame
> And bade self-love and social be the same. (III, 315-18)

Epistle IV is the concluding section. It is subtitled "Of the Nature and State of Man with Respect to Happiness". Having discussed man's relationship with the universe, in Epistle I, his relationship with himself as an individual, his relationship with society, Pope comes finally to his happiness. First, he discusses the false notions of happiness and refutes them. The opening paragraph is charged with emotion, unusual for the eighteenth century satirists. He says that happiness is the ultimate aim of every human being. It is called by different names like "good", "pleasure", "ease" and "contentment". People live for it and die for it. It is a plant grown of a "celestial seed". But it is ever present and yet ever elusive. It is elusive to those who do not know how to live and is gained by people like Lord Bolingbroke. If some people do not get happiness, they are at fault.

> If vain our toil,
> We ought to blame the culture, not the soil;
> Fixed to no spot is happiness sincere,
> 'Tis nowhere to be found, or everywhere,
> 'Tis never to be bought, but always free,
> And fled from monarchs, St. John! dwells with thee.
> (IV, 13-18)

The learned people do not know what happiness is. One scholar says that happiness lies in serving people and the other says that we can get true happiness by "shunning mankind".

Some men say that happiness is there in work but some men say that it is in indolence. Others speak of pleasure and contentment. Some people act like beasts to gain pleasure and end their life in pain and misery. Finally, a few people say that happiness cannot be defined.

Who thus define it, say they more or less
Than this, that happiness is happiness? (IV, 27-28)

Pope advises us to follow nature and shun meaningless ideas:

Take nature's path, and mad opinions leave;
All states can reach it, and all heads conceive;
Obvious her goods, in no extreme they dwell;
There needs but thinking right, and meaning well.
(IV, 29-32)

After this, he comes to the thesis he propounded in Epistle I.

Remember, man, the Universal Cause
Acts not by partial, but by general laws,
And makes what happiness we justly call
Subsists not in the good of one, but all. (IV, 35-39)

The emphasis is on common weal. Man must not be selfish. This is what God's law says. All pleasures get rotten and glories vanish if there is no one beside a man to share them. People of different status—fierce bandits, proud kings and hermits living in lonely caves—find that all that they have gained are fruitless as there is none to share with them. This world is ordered and everyone has got his right place. Therefore, it will be wrong to break the hierarchy. It is better to remain satisfied with the position a man lives in.

Order is heaven's first law; and this confest,
Some are, and must be, greater than the rest,
More rich, more wise; but who infers from hence
That such are happier, shocks all commonsense.
If all are equal in their happiness:
But mutual wants this happiness increase,

All nature's difference keeps all nature's peace.
Bliss is the same in subject or in king. (IV, 49-56)

The idea in line 56 is repeated in different words in lines 61-66:

Heaven breathes thro' every member of the whole
One common blessing, as one common soul,
But fortune's gifts if each alike possest,
And each were equal, must not all contest?
If then to all men happiness was meant,
God in externals could not place content.

Pope means to say that everything is ordered. If all people were given equal share of gifts by God, there would be a keen contest among them. In fact, fortune and happiness are two different things. Riches do not make a man happy. He says:

Know, all the good that individuals find,
Or God and nature meant to mere mankind,
Reason's whole pleasure, all the joys of sense,
Lie in three words, health, peace and competence
But health consists with temperance alone;
And peace, oh virtue! peace is all thy own. (IV, 77-82)

In God's scheme bliss and vice are contradictory and so are virtue and woe. Good people suffer but this does not mean that they are punished by God. Physical suffering is a part of nature. Even vicious people prosper. Earthly gains are not everything. A bad man may earn a lot of money by hard labour or by fraud. But riches do not make him virtuous. It may be said that sometimes the virtuous people starve and the wicked prosper. But if one asks virtuous man to have all the wealth and powers of a king, he will politely refuse. Virtue is supreme Pope says:

To whom can riches give repute, or trust,
Content, or pleasure, but the good and just?
Judges and senates have been bought for gold.
Esteem and love were never to be sold. (IV, 185-88)

Further,

> Honour and shame from no condition rise;
> Act well your part, there all the honour lies. (IV, 193-94)

Greatness and fame have little to do with happiness. Alexander of Macedonia, though called great, was only a mad man who killed a large number of people for his self-love Likewise,

> What is fame? a fancied life in others' breath,
> A thing beyond us, even before our death. (IV, 237-38)

A virtuous man makes a proper balance between self-love and reason. He knows that he is a social being and it is in sharing sorrow and joy of other people that he gets happiness. He is liked by the people around him. It is other people's love that gives us real happiness.

> Self-love thus pushed to social, to divine,
> Gives thee to make thy neighbour's blessing thine.
> (IV, 353-54)

If the seeker of happiness feels that the area of doing good is narrow, he can extend it to his enemies; let them also be recipients of his good deeds:

> Is this too little for the boundless heart?
> Extend it, let thy enemies have part,
> Grasp the whole worlds of reason, life and sense,
> In one close system of benevolence:
> Happier as kinder, in whatever degree
> And height of bliss but height of charity. (IV, 355-60)

God loves all. He moves from the general to the individual. Man should love but he must extend his self-love to love to all.

> God loves from whole to parts; but human soul
> Must rise from individual to whole. (IV, 361-62)

At the end of the Epistle, Pope pays tribute to St. John, Lord Bolingbroke, whom he calls his "guide, philosopher and friend" and says that he has written this poem at his behest. Then he gives the central idea of the Epistle:

That reason, passion, answer one great aim;
That true self-love and social are the same;
That virtue only makes our bliss below;
And all our knowledge is, ourselves to know.

(IV, 395-98)

Although called a theodicy by many critics, *An Essay on Man* is a searching analysis of man's nature and status in this world. Pope has rightly divided the poem into four sections, called epistles as they are addressed to Lord Bolingbroke, his friend, philosopher and guide, who inspired him to write this poem. It is certain that Bolingbroke's revolutionary philosophy moulded Pope's ideas and made him think over the meaning of life.

Pope follows Milton to a large extent. He does not hide his indebtedness but is more concerned with man in society. He accepts the idea of order, regularity, symmetry and harmony in God's system. He considers nature as God's creation which has a perfect system. Man, in order to achieve perfection, must follow nature. In *Essay on Criticism* he already had advised poets and critics to follow nature in writing poetry and evaluating it.

Here he extends this principle to total human life. Man should know what he is. He is a creation of God. He must not be unnatural, as nature, God's creation, is a perfect system Man has been given principles: the principle of self-love and the principle of reason. The principle of self-love is the motor force All actions of man are driven by self-love. But self-love may be misused. Therefore, there is the need of reason to guard it. Both are complementary to each other, and in their balanced fusion lies true happiness.

Notes

1. *Pope's Poetical Works,* "Introduction" to *Essay on Man*, p. 267.
2. G. Wilson Knight, *The Laureate of Peace*, p. 43.
3. Quoted. William Warburton, *Works of Pope,* p. 245.
4. *Ibid.*, p. 246.
5. Dustin H. Griffin, *Alexander Pope*, pp. 144-46.
6. *The Bible. Old Testament. Book of Job. Chapters 40 and 41.*
7. G. Wilson Knight, *The Laureate of Peace*, pp. 49-50.
8. Dustin H. Griffin, *op cit.*, pp. 32-33.

5

The Rape of the Lock

In *Essay on Criticism*, analysed in chapter III, Pope advises poets and critics to judge a poem by the author's intention. Although the New American Critics excluded intention from close analysis of a poem, most of the critics of the second half of the twentieth century are of the opinion that the author's intention as expressed in the created work is a vital point of study. Roland Barthes, a leading post-structuralist, considers intention to be of vital importance and so do the other post-structuralists.

If we read *The Rape of the Lock* carefully and seriously, we will find that it has been written in the light of the cardinal principles of order, regularity and harmony. It is a satire on the foppishness of the youth of aristocracy, who has deviated, from reason and nature and has become unnatural. The result is discord, strife and loss of peace.

The poem is an effort to bring the families of Robert Petre and Arabella Fermor to peace together. In one of his frolics, Lord Petre cut a lock of hair of Arabella Fermor. It was an outrageous act and it annoyed the young lady. It was more irksome for the reason that Lord Petre, a young man of twenty-two, loved her. A feud ensued between the two families as a result of this foolish act. John Caryll, a close relation of the Fermors suggested to Pope the idea of presenting the incident in a poem tinged with humour so that the two families will come to reconciliation. Pope, at first, refused to write such a poem. But, later on, took up the matter and wrote the first version of *The Rape of the*

Lock in 314 lines. There were two cantos only. After some time he worked further on it and enlarged it to five cantos.

Why did he do so? He refused it first and then wrote and rewrote? The answer is that Pope did not want to be an ordinary poet. Well-educated and highly rational, he fitted the incident in his own scheme of writing poetry. He had already written *Essay on Criticism* in which he had explained his theory and practice of poetic art. Besides, he wanted to purge the two families of their pride and aberration from nature (reason) in a humorous way. As the two families belonged to aristocracy, he chose the mock heroic form. *The Rape of the Lock*, therefore, should be read as a poem that exemplifies Pope's concept of the relationship between nature and art. G. Wilson Knight comments:

> Shakespeare gives us drama and Milton epic, and Pope builds from both in *The Rape of the Lock* (1712-14). The poem has Lyly's feeling for the delightfully evanescent, the poignant attractiveness of a brilliant society. Yet Lyly offered no strong action, and against this subtlest of poetic problems Pope very early pits his genius, preserving the essence of heroic poetry on condition of a semi-humorous treatment.[1]

Britannica Ready Reference Encyclopaedia defines the epic that it is a

> long, narrative poem in an elevated style that celebrates heroic achievement and treats themes of historical, national, religious or legendary significance. Primary (or traditional) epics are shaped from the legends and traditions of a heroic age and are part of oral tradition; secondary (or literary) epics are written down from the beginning, and their poets adapt aspects of traditional epics.
>
> (*Britannica Ready Reference Encyclopaedia*, Vol. III, p. 256)

Homer's *Iliad* and *Odyssey*, Valmiki's *Ramayana* and Vyasa's *Mahabharata* are the most famous primary epics. Milton's *Paradise Lost* is a literary epic. The literary epic follows the conventions of the primary epic. The main conventions are:

1. Stylistic
   (a) An invocation to a god or goddess who is the patron of poetry and the fine arts.
   (b) Use of Homeric simile.
   (c) Use of the heroic couplet.
2. Thematic
   (a) The central figure is a hero—Achilles in *Iliad*, Odysseus in *Odyssey*, Rama in the *Ramayana* and Arjuna in the *Mahabharata*.
   (b) The setting is extensive, almost cosmic.
   (c) There is a heroic battle.
   (d) There is, at least, one extended or long journey.
   (e) There is the involvement of supernatural beings.

The mock-heroic parodies the epic. So far the style and technique are concerned, it follows the epic loosely but when the theme and characters come, it just goes opposite of the loftiness and sublimity of the epic. The subject matter is trivial and the characters fools. When Pope began writing, he did not take the poem seriously because the subject matter was ephemeral. But, later on he gave a serious thought to it and fitted it in his theory of nature and art. A close analysis of the poem will show his intention and deft handling of the matter.

The poem begins with an invocation to the Muse, goddess of poetry. But the addition of the names of John Caryll and Belinda (Arabella Fermor) makes his intention clear; he wants to reconcile the two families who are quarrelling over a trifling matter. The wrath of Achilles and the other Greek heroes was flamed by the humiliation they suffered at the hands of Paris, a prince of Troy. Here, there is no such cause; it is only a storm in a tea cup.

> What dire offence from amorous causes springs
> What mighty contests rise from trivial things,
> I sing—This verse to Caryll, Muse! is due:
> This even Belinda may vouchsafe to view.
>
> (Canto I, 1-4)

The lines 7-12 have the eloquence of an epic. The style is sublime:

> Say what strange motive, goddess! could compel
> A well bred lord to assault a gentle belle?
> O say what stranger cause, yet unexplored,
> Could make a gentle belle reject a lord?
> In tasks so bold, can little men engage
> And in soft bosoms dwells such mighty rage?
>
> (Canto I, 7-12)

The rhetorical questions are answers in themselves. The first two lines deprecate Lord Petre's behaviour. The poet is unable to find out the cause for cutting Belinda's hair. After all it is an absurd and indecent act. In the same vein he expresses his surprise at Belinda's behaviour of rejecting her lover, Robert Petre. And after the event, it is surprising that a lady like Belinda (Arabella Fermor) should have so much of rage in her soft and compassionate heart. We find here that Pope starts making a peaceful reconciliation between the two by hitting at the truth that the act was no doubt shameful and below the dignity of a gentleman, but Belinda's reaction, too was not becoming of her. This invocation fits in his theory of poetry of nature and art. Both Petre and Fermor have deviated from nature and what Pope is doing is to correct them and make them go the natural way.

After the invocation, we are led to Belinda's bedroom. Here, Pope ridicules the excessive fashion and artificiality of the rich people of his time. Their total life is rather unnatural. Belinda is sleeping in her bed. The sun rises and its rays enter her bedroom through the curtain. The poet has used the phrase "a timorous ray" to show Belinda's pride and quick temper. The ray is timorous, not bold to enter her room. It is quite late. We know that Belinda is a late riser through these lines:

> Now lap-dogs give themselves the rousing shake,
> And sleepless lovers, just at twelve awake.
>
> (Canto I, 15-16)

It follows then that Belinda rises at 12 o'clock in day when the sun's rays enter her room and the lap dogs shake their own body and the maidservant presses the alarm bell of the watch.

In spite of all that Belinda is still resting and recollecting her dream at night.

It is here that the supernatural element is introduced. In a heroic poem, the supernatural elements are the powerful gods who help their proteges and take revenge on those people who have insulted them. Since *The Rape of the Lock* is a mock-heroic poem and Pope's aim is to evoke laughter and correct the unnaturalness of the young people by means of humour, the supernatural elements are the sylphs. He explains the characteristics of the sylphs whom he calls the machinery.

> The machinery, Madam* is a term invented by the critics to signify that part which the Deities, Angels, or Daemons are made to act in a poems for the ancient poets are in one respect like many modern ladies: let an action be never so trivial in itself, they always make it appear of the utmost importance. These machines I determined to raise on a very new and odd foundation, the Rosicrucian doctrine of spirits.
>
> I know how disagreeable it is to make use of hard words before a lady; but 'tis so much the concern of a poet to have his works understood, and particularly by your sex, that you must give me leave to explain two or three difficult terms.
>
> The Rosicrucians are a people I must bring you acquainted with. The best account I know of them is in a French book called *Le Comte de Gabalis*, which, both in its title and size, is so like a novel that many of the fair sex have read it for one by mistake. According to these gentlemen, the four elements are inhabited by spirits which they call, Sylphs, Gnomes, Nymphs, and Salamanders. The Gnomes, or Daemons of Earth delight in mischief but the Sylphs, whose habitation is in the air, are the best-conditioned creatures imaginable. For they say any mortals may enjoy the most intimate familiarities with these gentle spirits, upon a condition very easy to all true adepts, an inviolate preservation of Chastity.[2]

* "Madam" is Arabella Fermor.

As presented in the poem the sylphs are very tiny, much smaller than the inhabitants of Liliput in Swift's *Gulliver's Travels*. Ariel who is the leader of the sylphs comes to Belinda in her dream and tells about the different spirits. He, like the Greek goddesses, is the patron of Belinda and takes utmost care for her welfare. He knows the impending calamity that is going to befall next day. He warns her of the danger:

> In the clear mirror of thy ruling star
> I saw, alas! some dread event impend,
> Ere to the main this morning sun descend
> But heaven reveals not what, or how, or where:
> Warned by the sylph, oh, pious maid beware!
> This to disclose is all thy guardian can:
> Beware of all, but most beware of man!"
>
> (Canto I, 108-14)

But before giving her the warming signal, he introduces himself and it is in his introduction that we learn the excessive idle and luxurious life of the aristocracy in the eighteenth century and in our age of democracy realize the gulf between the lives of the hard working labourers and peasants and the rich big landlords. Pope with a subtle irony ridicules the excessive luxury and pompous fashion of the rich people.

After introducing himself Ariel asks her to remember the fairy stories she heard in her childhood. The stories tell about the angels and fairies that visit the small children. They wear golden crown and heavenly flowers that never fade. He tells Belinda that the angels, fairies and elves are not imaginary people. On the other hand, they are real. He says:

> Hear and believe! thy own importance know,
> Nor bound thy narrow views to things below
> Some secret truths, from learned pride concealed,
> To maids alone and children are revealed.
>
> (Canto I, 35-38)

He continues to tell that there are countless spirits flying round her. They are the "light militia" of the lower sky. They hang over the perfume boxes, hang by the golden rings worn by ladies and fly over beautiful ladies. After this comes the scathing criticism of the excessive fashion of the aristocratic ladies of the eighteenth century. Ariel says that they become salamander after their death.

Think not, when women's transient breath is fled,
That all her vanities at once are dead;
Succeeding vanities she still regards,
And though she plays no more overlooks the cards.
Her joy in golden chariots when alive,
And love of ombre, after death survive.
For when the fair in all their pride expire,
To their first elements their souls retire;
The sprites of fiery termagants in flame
Mount up, and take a Salamander's name.

(Canto I, 51-60)

The other fairies are gnomes. They are prudes and mischievous:

The graver prude sinks downward to a gnome,
In search of mischief still on earth to roam.
The light coquettes in sylphs aloft repair,
And sport and flutter in the fields of air.

(Canto I, 63-66)

Since the sylphs are the spirits of the fashionable ladies, they help the ladies on the earth in many ways. It is also that the sylphs have not forgotten the pleasures of their previous life. Naturally, they oversee the different games played by ladies. Sometimes, they guide ladies to preserve their chastity. Ariel says:

When Florio speaks, what virgins could withstand,
If gentle Damon did not squeeze her hand?
With varying vanities, from every part
They shift the moving toy-shop of their heart;
Where wigs with wigs, with sword-knots sword-knots strive
Beaux banish beaux, and coaches coaches drive.

This erring mortals! levity may call,
Oh, blind to truth! the sylphs contrive it all.

(Canto I, 97-104)

This speech of Ariel is full of humour. Through him, Pope describes the vain life of the young lords and ladies of the time. Besides, the haughty speech of Ariel exposes his own weakness. He is not Shakespeare's Ariel in *The Tempest*. Ariel in *The Tempest* is very powerful but Pope's Ariel is too tiny and though he boasts of his power, we know that he is powerless. Thus, his speech creates humour also. The dream is over and Ariel is gone and yet Belinda is sleeping. Her dog, Shock, feels that she has slept too long. He goes to her and wakes her by licking her. The beautiful lady wakes and looks at the love-letter printed nicely. Seeing the charming billet-doux she forgets her dream and the warning. She goes to her toilet. The description is brilliant. Professor G. Wilson Knight is of the opinion that religious and the erotic are mingled together for the reader's amusement. He writes:

> By seeing Belinda's toilet preparations as a ritual the poet channels reverend associations that build his scene and its action into both a more convincing and a more memorable impressionistic whole than would otherwise be possible. Nor is this merely a technical fancy, since the religion of post-Renaissance literature is, fundamentally, an Eros cult. So, in blending religious terms with feminine vanity, Pope makes a synthesis of the Christianity-Eros conflict on a comparatively superficial, but delightfully human plane, the rich humour being both the measure of a relation and the resolving of a conflict.[3]

In fact, Pope has wonderfully woven the threads of religion and feminine beauty. The first four lines appear as if they are describing the inner part of a temple:

And now, unveiled, the toilet stands displayed,
Each silver vase in mystic order laid.
First, robed in white, the Nymph intent adores,
With head uncovered, the cosmetic powers.

(Canto I, 12-15)

The words "unveiled", "mystic order", "adores", "robed in white" and "head uncovered" are indicative of worship in a temple. Generally, there is a curtain in the inner part of a temple or Church. The priestess wearing a white dress enters the Church. She uncovers her head out of reverence. There are censors in the inner part for worshipping and burning incense. Here Belinda is described as a priestess in the toilet. The toilet looks like a temple where the worshipper stands robed in white. There is a deft use of parallelism. But there is humour also. When we read the phrase "cosmetic powers" we are reminded of the phrase "Cosmic powers". We smile at the similarity in sound and contrast in meaning. The subsequent lines expand the idea:

A heavenly image in the glass appears,
To that she bends, to that her eyes she rears;
The inferior priestess, at her altar's side,
Trembling begins the sacred rites of pride.

(Canto I, 25-28)

The heavenly image is, of course, that of Belinda. In fact, Arabella Fermor was a well-known beauty of her society. The inferior priestess is Betty, her maidservant. Here, Pope has very adroitly introduced the word "pride". The literal meaning is that Belinda sits before the life-size mirror for her make-up. Betty is there to assist her. Belinda's image is reflected in the mirror. The irony is introduced by means of the word "pride". Belinda is proud of her beauty. But pride leads to a person's fall. Here no goddess is worshipped nor is there the Christian humility. Belinda's pride will lead her to misery. This goddess is not inferior to any goddess. On the other hand, she is more respected. Offerings come to her from all the corners of the world. The offerings are the richest:

Unnumbered treasures ope at once, and here
The various offerings of the world appear;
From each she nicely culls with curious toil,
And decks the goddess with the glittering spoil.
This casket India's glowing gems unlocks,
And all Arabia breathes from yonder box.

The tortoise here and elephant unite,
Transformed to combs the speckled and the white.

(Canto I, 129-36)

Then Belinda, helped by Betty, completes her make-up:

Now awful beauty puts on all its arms;
The fair each moment rises in her charms,
Repairs her smiles, awakens every grace,
And calls forth all the wonders of her face.

(Canto I, 139-42)

The description of Belinda's toilet is one of the finest in English poetry. G. Wilson Knight comments:

> The whole passage is, to use the fine term applied by A.C. Bradley to the poetry of Keats, 'dense'. There is nothing visually flat. Pope is not a pre-eminently visual poet; rather he tells facts, names concrete objects, attaches needed epithets. But his reserve attains great richness, and his epithets modify with precision and force, as in the adjective 'mystic' both helping the main analogy and underlining the maid's professional care to serve a realistic purpose. The sacramental associations concretize, and give depth to, the whole business; objects are made alive, till they breathe out significant energy.[4]

The first Canto rightly opens *The Lock*. The poem is mock-heroic in the Augustan sense, not a common parody. Professor Ian Jack writes in *The Augustan Satire*:

> In mock-epic a dignified genre is turned to witty use without being cheapened in any way. The poet has an opportunity of ridiculing incongruity, and of affording his reader the sophisticated pleasure of recognizing ironical parallels to familiar passages in Homer and Virgil. A mock-heroic poem is a "parody" of the epic, but a parody in the Augustan sense, not in the modern. The "new purpose" of the frequent "allusions" through *The Rape of the Lock* is not the ridicule of a literary form but the setting of a lover's tiff in true perspective.[5]

The invocation in the opening lines is serious and the use of the heroic couplet is perfect. Even the passage where humour is dominant, there is no cheapness. Bathos and Zeugma are deftly used. The introduction of the supernatural and its treatment is superb. Just as the main passion of *Iliad* is anger and tender passion in *Aeneid* coquetry is the reigning passion of *The Rape of the Lock*. Pride is connected with coquetry. Pope found the Rosicrucian doctrine suitable for the poem and this is because of the erotic quality of the sylphs that Professor Jack writes:

> ...in Pope's poem they figure primarily as the allies of women in their unceasing war with mankind. Nor did Pope find in *de Gobalis* more than the slightest hints towards the airy beauty of his supernatural beings. The main thing that he took over was merely the licence to invent a fantastic race whose presence would make every trivial incident in his poem appear of the utmost importance. The sylphs are the mirrors added to his scene. By them the central action is reflected and multiplied a hundredfold, gaining in subtlety and mystery as well as in ironical importance.[6]

II

Canto II is dominated by sylphs. Pope's description of their activities is superb. We are simply amused. The region of the sylphs is air. The poet has very artistically led us to water where our nymph Belinda sits in a beautifully decorated boat in the Thames. The opening lines are:

> Not with more glories, in the ethereal plain
> The sun first rise over the purpled main,
> Than issuing forth, the rival of his beams
> Launched on the bossom of the silver Thames.
>
> (Canto II, 1-4)

In the shining boat is Belinda sitting surrounded by other beautiful belles but everybody's eyes are fixed on her. She is depicted thus:

> On her white breast a sparkling cross she wore,
> Which Jews might kiss, and infidels adore.
>
> (Canto II, 7-8)

Bright as the sun, her eyes the gazers strike
And like the sun, they shine on all alike
Yet graceful ease, and sweetness void of pride,
Might hide her faults, if belles had faults to hide;
If to her share some female errors fall,
Look on her face, and you'll forget them all.

(Canto II, 13-18)

After this comes the description of her hair:

This nymph, to the destruction of mankind,
Nourished two locks, which gracefully hung behind
In equal curls, and well conspired to deck
With shining ringlets, the smooth ivory neck.

(Canto II, 19-22)

The locks of hair have special qualities. They are beautiful and highly attractive and capable of ensnaring the beholder's look. Here the sublime and the comic are yoked together. Pope has the ability to use irony of the subtlest kind. He describes the trivial in a grand style for humour:

Love in these labyrinth his slaves detains,
And mighty hearts are held in slender chains.
With hairy springs we the birds betray
Slight lines of hair surprise the finny prey,
Fair tresses man's imperial race ensnare
And beauty draws us with a single hair.

(Canto II, 23-28)

After describing Belinda boating in the Thames, Pope takes us to Lord Petre. Here, humour is at its best. Arabella Fermor must have laughed heartily after reading this passage. Enamoured with Belinda's enticing locks, the Baron wishes to have them. For this he worships the god of love:

For this, ere Phoebus rose, he had implored
Propitious Heaven, and every power adored.
But Chiefly Love—to love an altar built
Of twelve vast French romances, neatly gilt.

(Canto II, 36-39)

The way he bows to his god tickles us to laughter:

With tender billet-doux he lights the pyre,
And breathes three amorous sighs to raise the fire.
Then prostrate falls, and begs with ardent eyes
Soon to obtain, and long possess the prize.

(Canto II, 41-44)

The next two lines end his worship with pure humour:

The powers gave ear, and granted half his prayer,
The rest, the winds dispersed in empty air.

(Canto II, 45-46)

Pope's wit is brilliant. Further we are vaguely told that he will get only one lock, not the both. The focus soon shifts from Petre to Belinda in a gilded boat in the Thames.

But now secure the painted vessel glides,
The sun beams trembling on the floating tides;
While melting music steals upon the sky,
And softened sounds along the water die.

(Canto II, 47-50)

All the friends of Belinda are joyful and so is Belinda. The only sad person is Ariel who knows the future; the impending woe sits heavy on his breast. He, therefore, summons all his denizens to come to the boat and help Belinda. The sylphs do every kind of act to make Belinda's boating on the Thames very pleasant. The display of colours is beautifully described:

Loose to the wind their airy garments flew,
Thin glittering textures of the filmy dew,
Dipped in the richest tincture of the skies,
Where light disports in ever mingling dyes
While every beam new transient colours flings
Colours that change whenever they wave their wings.

(Canto II, 63-68)

Such colour is only one aspect of the beauty which Pope describes. Throughout the poem the senses are flattered as delicately as they are in Belinda's world itself. It is fitting that the punishments inflicted on negligent sylphs should be the quintessence of the torture of senses. Such a sinner, Ariel warns and through him the moralist poet:

Shall feel sharp vengeance soon overtake his sins,
Be stopped in vials, or transfixed with pins;
Or plunged in lakes of bitter washes lie,
Or wedged whole ages in a bodkin's eye;
Gums and pomatums shall his flight restrain,
While clogged he beats his silken wings in vain:
Or alum styptics with contracting power
Shrink his thin essence like a riveted flower;
Or as Ixion fixed, the wretch shall feel
The giddy notion of the whirling wheel.

(Canto II, 125-34)

Canto II ends with Ariel's warning. The sylphs listen to him and get themselves busy in the protection of Belinda but are apprehensive of the coming danger.

With beating hearts the dire event they wait,
Anxious and trembling for the birth of Fate.

(Canto II, 141-42)

III

In Canto III, the rape of the lock is done. The poem, though a mock-epic, is structured like a drama. The first Canto is the exposition, the second complication, the third climax, the fourth anti-climax and the fifth conclusion. Young men and women assemble in Hampton, a royal house, for pleasure in the afternoon when the rays of the sun are in the declining stage. Pope adds spice to the opening of the Canto by his wit. The use of Zeugma makes these lines perfect in wit:

Here Britain's statesmen oft the fall foredoom
Of foreign tyrants, and of nymphs at home;
Here thou, great Anna! whom three realms obey
Dost sometimes counsel take and some times tea.

(Canto III, 5-8)

The poet contrives to unite the epic convention of war and the battle of cards in the game named ombre very adroitly. In the *Iliad,* there is the Trojan war and the *Odyssey* has a series of battles. Here, the battle is between Belinda and Lord Petre. This is not a battle in the real sense. It is the battle in the game of ombre. Ombre was a popular game at cards in the eighteenth century. Its place has been taken by other kinds of the game.

The game played by the two adversaries is narrated as if a battle is being fought. The battlefield is a triangular table. Each player has her/his cards. Just as a general surveys his army, Belinda throws a glance at the cards consisting of aces, kings, queens and jacks or knaves:

> Belinda now, whom thirst of fame invites,
> Burns to encounter two adventurous knights,
> At ombre singly to decide their doom;
> And swells her breast with conquests yet to come.
>
> (Canto III, 25-28)

and then "The skilful nymph reviews her force with care" (Canto III, 45) like a general of the army.

Just as Homer has described the armies of Greece and Troy and Ved Vyasa of the Kauravas and the Pandavas, Pope presents the armies of Belinda and Petre. The total effect is comic. Whereas the heroes in the epics are real persons, the kings in *The Rape of the Lock* are paper-kings. The description is grand and reminds us of Milton's grand style:

> Behold, four kings in majesty revered
> With hoary whiskers and a forky beard.
>
> (Canto III, 37-38)

Soon we come to know that they are pictures on cards:

> And four fair queens, whose hands sustain a flower,
> The expressive emblem of their softer power;
> Four knaves in garbs succinct, a trusty band;
> Caps on their hands and halberts in their hand
> And partly coloured troops, a shining train
> Drawn forth to combat on the velvet plain.
>
> (Canto III, 39-44)

The greatest comic effect is made through this couplet:

> The skilful nymph reviews her force with care;
> Let spades be trumps! she said, and they were.
>
> (Canto III, 45-46)

The use of bathos is remarkable. The second line of the couplet reminds us of the Genesis in the Bible: "And God said, 'Let there be light!' and there was light." We burst into laughter after reading the line. The humour is pure and unmalicious.

The war begins after the declaration. The battle is fierce. But at every place Belinda has the upper hand. Pope has described the battle of the paper heroes in great detail. The details must have amused the eighteenth century people who played ombre with great enthusiasm. At last, Belinda wins the game. She is jubilant. She shouts. Her shout is so loud that the surroundings vibrate:

> The nymph exulting fills with shouts the sky;
> The Walls, the woods, and long canals reply.
>
> (Canto III, 99-100)

But she does not know the impending danger. It is said that pride goeth before a fall. She, too, should not have elated so much. Here is the poet's commentary:

> O thoughtless mortals! ever blind to fate,
> Too soon dejected, and too soon elate.
> Sudden, these honours shall be snatched away,
> And cursed for ever this victorious day.
>
> (Canto III, 101-04)

The game is over. Now it is coffee-time. The servants bring coffee in gorgeous vessels. The description of grinding the baked coffee-seeds and the making of coffee is really wonderful. How coffee is served is tantalisingly described:

> The berries crackle, and the mill turns round
> On shining altars of Japan they raise
> The silver lamp; the fiery spirits blaze:
> From silver spouts the grateful liquors glide,
> While China's earth receives the smoking tide.
>
> (Canto III, 106-10)

In those days the instant coffee was not in vogue. Even today, people of fine taste roast the seeds, grind them and with the newly ground powder make coffee. In fact, this method is the best method of preparing coffee.

The coffee has a strange effect on Petre, the kind of effect it has on politicians. Politicians become wise under its influence and begin to see everything shutting their eyes. Petre, too, begins to see a new strategy to gain Belinda's tantalizing locks.

> Coffee (which makes the politician wise,
> And see through all things with his half-shut eyes)
> Sent up in vapours to the baron's brain
> New stratagems, the radiant lock to gain.
>
> (Canto III, 117-20)

In the true epic style, the poet warns the baron:

> Ah cease, rash youth! desist ere 'tis too late,
> Fear the just gods, and think of Scylla's fate!
> Changed to a bird, and sent to flit in air
> She dearly pays for Nisus' injured hair!

This reference to Ovid's *Metamorphoses* is quite apt and in the tradition of a serious epic. Nisus, the king of Megara, had a purple lock of hair on the top of his head among the honourable silver. His daughter, Scylla, saw Minos, the Cretan invader, from the watch-tower and fell in love with him. She desired that Minos would conquer her country and make her his wife. For this, she cut the purple lock from her father's head and gave it to Minos. She told that her father could not be defeated so long the purple lock was on his head. But Minos got disgusted with her selfishness and sailed back home. Scylla, because of her selfishness and treachery, was changed into an osprey. Here the ancient myth is referred to dissuade Petre from doing the rash and selfish act of cutting Belinda's beautiful lock of hair.

But Petre remains adamant. He is supported by Clarissa in the mischief. She brings a pair of scissors and presents it to him. Now fully armed, he goes on for knight-errantry as if he would win laurels for cutting the lock. Pope describes the incident:

The peer now spreads the glittering forfex wide,
To enclose the lock; now join it, to divide.
Fate urged the shears, and cut...
The meeting points the sacred hair dissever
From the fair head, for ever, and for ever!

(Canto III, 147-48, 151, 153-54)

Soon Belinda comes to know the cutting of her hair. Her reaction is of surprise and horror. Unable to bear the insult, she falls in a rage:

Then flashed the living lightening from her eyes,
And screams of horror rend the affrighted skies.
Not louder shrieks to pitying Heaven are cast,
When husbands or when lap-dogs breathe their last.

(Canto III, 155-58)

Here Pope's craftsmanship is at its best. The reaction of Belinda is quite natural and she is really angry and horrified. Her shriek must have been loud and piercing. Pope uses hyperbole to depict her horror and anger. But he does not allow it to be a tragic situation. He uses bathos and zeugma for the comic effect. We fall lightly from the height of lines 155-57 to the last line of the quoted passage. We cannot control our laughter when husbands and lap-dogs are given equal importance by the fashionable ladies. The next two lines complete the comic effect:

Or when rich China vessels, fallen from high,
In glittering dust and painted fragments lie.

(Canto III, 159-60)

Lord Petre is jubilant. He is happy over his great victory. He proclaims:

Let wreaths of triumph now my temples twine,
(The victor cried) the glorious prize is mine
While fish in streams, or birds delight in air,
Or in a coach and six the British fair
As long as Atalantis shall be read
Or the small pillow grace a lady's bed,

While visits shall be paid on solemn days,
When numerous wax-lights in bright order blaze,
While nymphs take treats, or assignations give,
So long my honour, name, and praise shall live!

(Canto III, 161-70)

There cannot be more comic similes. It is Pope's great quality that he suggests humour in the most stately words.

Canto IV tells us Umbriel's visit to the underworld. In the epic tradition, there is the visit to the underworld, the Hades. Pope imitates the tradition. But the dark sinister underworld is not ruled by Hades or Pluto but by Spleen.

The cutting of the lock of hair enrages Belinda first but when she finds that the loss is irreparable and she cannot do anything, she falls in a gloom. She is morose and dejected. The poet counts a number of instances and then concludes:

(None) ever felt such rage, resentment, and despair,
As thou, sad virgin! for thy ravished hair.

(Canto IV, 9-10)

At this moment of gloom, Ariel leaves the place weeping. But to add more woe to Belinda, Umbriel, a melancholy sprite, comes to her to intensify her woe. He is a sprite of darkness and gloom. Now, he is happy that at least there is a person in this world who can be his choice. He makes a journey to the Cave of Spleen from where he can bring potions to increase Belinda's sorrow. The Cave and Spleen are described thus:

No cheerful breeze this sullen region knows,
The dreaded east is all the wind that blows.
Here in a grotto, sheltered close from air
And screened in shades from day's detested glare
She sighs for ever on tier pensive bed
Pain at her side, and Megrim at her head.

(Canto IV, 20-25)

The two attendants are equally gloomy. The first handmaid is ill-nature and the second is affectation with a sickly mien. There is a constant vapour rising from the palace. The vapour takes the forms of phantoms. The phantoms are those of expiring maids, glaring friends, snakes on rolling spires, pale ghosts, gaping tombs and purple fires. We are amused with this description. Then we laugh loudly after reading the following lines. The use of bathos is masterly. We marvel at Pope's twist of expectations for producing humour.

> Unnumbered throngs on every side are seen
> Of bodies changed to various forms by Spleen
> Here living tea-pots stand, one arm hold out
> One bent; the handle this, and that the spout:
> A pipkin there, like Homer's tripod walks
> Here sighs a jar, and there a goose-pie talks.
>
> (Canto III, 48-53)

Umbriel enters the cave and reaches Spleen and requests her to give a potion to augment Belinda's grief. But before making the request he addresses her reverently:

> Hail, wayward Queen!
> Who rule the sex to fifty from fifteen;
> Parent of vapours, and of female wit,
> Who give the hysteric or poetic fit. (Canto III, 57-60)

The goddess listens to his prayer. Like a snobbish woman she seems to reject the prayer but, in fact, grants it and gives him a wonderful bag which is comparable to the bag given to Ulysses.

The bag of Ulysses contained winds. Here different potions are kept in the bag. The potions will aggravate Belinda's sorrow:

> A wondrous bag with both her hands she binds,
> Like that where once Ulysses held the wind
> There she collects the force of female lungs,
> Sighs, sobs, and passions, and the war of tongues
> A vial next she fills with fainting fears,
> Soft sorrows, melting griefs and flowing tears.
>
> (Canto III, 81-86)

Umbriel takes the bag and flies quickly to Belinda. He spares no time in breaking open the vials and pouring the potions on her. The medicines have magic effect:

> Then see! the nymph in beauteous grief appears,
> Her eyes half-languishing, half-drowned in tears.
> On her heaved bosom hung her drooping head.
>
> (Canto III, 144-46)

Now she laments:

> For ever cursed be this detested day,
> Which snatched my best, my favourite curl away!
> Happy! ay, ten times happy had I been
> If Hampton Court these eyes had never seen!
> Yet I am not the first mistaken maid
> By love of Courts to numerous ills betrayed,
> Oh had I rather unadmired remained
> In some love isle, or distant northern land
> Where the gilt chariot never marks the way
> Where none learn ombre, none ever taste bohea!
> There kept my charms concealed from mortal eye,
> Like roses that in deserts bloom and die.
>
> (Canto III, 147-58)

Belinda's lament moves us. The last six lines are a kind of penitence. Besides, they are a critical commentary on the foolish entertainment of the young people of aristocracy. The last line in the quoted passage "Like roses that in deserts bloom and die" perhaps inspired Thomas Gray to write these immortal lines in "Elegy Written in a Country Churchyard".

> Full many a flower is born to blush unseen
> And waste its sweetness on the desert air.

Canto V is the concluding part of the poem. It begins with the effect of Belinda's lament. People are rather stunned but recover soon to console her. As it is a mock-epic, Pope describes the situation with a tinge of humour:

> She said: the pitying audience melt in tears;
> But Fate and Love had stopped the baron's ears.
>
> (Canto V, 1-2)

Seeing that Petre is unmoved, Belinda speaks in reproachful words:

> Say, why are beauties praised and honoured most,
> The wise man's passion, and the vain man's toast?
>
> (Canto V, 9-10)

In her long speech, she goes on laying emphasis on the tradition of ladies' efforts to look beautiful and win men's hearts. She also takes the help of *carpe diem* when she says that frail beauty has to decay and the bright locks will turn grey some day. But her words have no effect on the audience. She is now desperate. Now the anger of Achilles enters her soul. Like Achilles, she asks for arms to fight with her adversary. Once, she takes the initiative, a battle ensues:

> All side in parties, and begin the attack:
> Fans clap, silks rustle, and tough whalebones crack,
> Heroes' and heroines' shouts confusedly rise,
> And bass and treble voices strike the skies,
> No common weapons in their hands are found,
> Like gods they fight, nor dread a mortal wound.
>
> (Canto V, 39-44)

The poet humorously comments on the fight in Hampton Court:

> So when bold Homer makes the gods engage,
> And heavenly breasts with human passions rage;
> 'Gainst Pollas, Mars; Latona, hermes arms
> And all Olympus rings with loud alarms
> Jove's thunder mars, Heaven trembles all around,
> Blue Neptune storms, the bellowing deeps resound.
>
> (Canto V, 45-50)

Making use of exaggeration or hyperbole Pope laughs at the petty quarrel of the fops. Pope once said that humour lies in describing trifling things in a stately language. And this is what he has done in comparing the situation with the war of gods at Mount Olympus.

The fight between Belinda and Petre is continued further. It is the convention of the classical epic that Jupiter takes the scale and weighs the chances of the warring heroes. Here, too Jove takes the scale and weighs the chances of Belinda and Petre:

> Now Jove suspends his golden scales in air
> Weighs the men's wits against the lady's hair;
> The doubtful beam long nods from side to side;
> At length the wits mount up, the hairs subside.
>
> (Canto V, 71-74)

Here the trifling and the heroic are yoked together to create humour. Besides, the last line is full of wit.

The scale of Petre goes up and that of Belinda goes down. But the meaning is that the scale shows Belinda's victory. Arabella must have laughed after reading these lines:

> See fierce Belinda on the baron flies,
> With more than unusual lightning in her eyes
> Nor feared the chief the unequal fight to try,
> Who sought no more than on his foe to die
> But this bold lord with manly strength endued
> She with one finger and a thumb subdued.
>
> (Canto V, 75-80)

The fight of course is comic. Belinda throws a pinchful of snuff on the face of the baron:

> Sudden, with starting tears each eye overflows
> And the high dome re-echoes to his nose.
>
> (Canto V, 84-85)

The baron, after seeing his poor defeat, says to Belinda:

> Boast not my fall, (he cried) insulting foe!
> Thou by some other shalt be laid as low.
> Nor think, to die dejects my lofty mind:
> All that I dread is leaving you behind!
>
> (Canto V, 97-100)

It seems that the baron has lost the ground but the last two lines make a somersault, he expresses his love:

> Rather than so, ah let me still survive,
> And burn in Cupid's flowers—but burn alive.
>
> (Canto V, 101-02)

But Belinda is relentless and demands her lock. The poet humorously compares the loudness and ferocity of her voice with that of Othello when he demanded his handkerchief. But the lock is not in the possession of the baron; it has gone to the stars as ordained by Heaven:

> But trust the Muse—she saw it upward rise,
> Though marked by none but quick, poetic eyes:
> A sudden star it shot through liquid air,
> And drew behind a radiant trail of hair,
> Not Berenice's lock first rose so bright.
> The heavens bespangling with dishevelled light.
>
> (Canto V, 123-24; 127-30)

The Rape of the Lock is an attempt to bring back order and harmony in society at the family level. Feuds arise out of irrationality. Lord Petre's act was irrational, hence unnatural. His act brought disorder and discord. But Belinda and her family overacted. After all Petre loved her and, the aristocratic society as it was in those days, frolics and foppery went hand in hand. Pope as advised by John Carryl wrote the poem to establish peace and order in the two families and save the embarrassment of the common friends.

While making his final estimate of *The Rape of the Lock,* Professor Ian Jack considers its moral highly. He writes:

> The moral of *The Rape of the Lock* must not be forgotten. If he meant to include the poem amongst the early work in which pure description held the place of sense, Pope was being deliberately unfair. *The Rape of the Lock* is itself the best evidence that "sense" may be expressed by means of a fable and made more vivid by narrative and description. For all his delight in the beauty of Belinda's world Pope never allows it to arrogate the place which rightly belongs to the sovereignty of sense.[7]

After making this statement, he quotes the last twenty lines of Canto I and then comments:

> Pope delights in the artificial beauty that he is describing. Yet he passes a judgement, which is expressed by the imagery of the whole passage. Just as Ben Jonson makes Vulpine condemn himself out of his own month by apostrophizing

> Gold in idolatrous terms so in the description of the toilet-table Pope shows Belinda lavishing on her own beauty the adoration of which should be reserved for a higher object. Pope acknowledges the beauty of the scene, and points it brilliantly; yet he reminds the reader that the rites he is describing are those "Of Pride". In the thought of the eighteenth century pride remained the first of sins. By making it "sacred" Belinda, and the whole *bean monde* which she represents is guilty of a serious moral fault.[8]

As discussed in the first chapter, God for the people of the eighteenth century was Supreme and nature and art were to follow Him. To be irrational was to go against nature. The prime cause of aberration was pride. As both Belinda and the Baron and their class suffer from vanity and pride, they become irrational and break the order, regularity and symmetry of the society.

Pope's greatness lies in making a smooth and harmonious relation between man on one hand and nature and God on the other. The subject matter of the poem is the stupid act of Lord Petre. A minor poet would have made it a humorous poem and created some fun but as G. Wilson Knight has pointed out Pope's treatment of the theme is serious and humane. He creates humour, no doubt, but what is significant is that he makes a kind of reconciliation between the two young persons; his aim is to establish peace and harmony at the family level, the basic unit of a society. He does not glorify either Lord Petre or Belinda (Arabella Fermor). He rather ridicules them and makes fun of their idiosyncracies. His moral judgement runs throughout the poem.

Notes

1. G. Wilson Knight, *Laureate of Peace*, p. 22.
2. "Dedication to Miss Arabella Fermor". *Works*, p. 351.
3. G. William Knight, p. 23.
4. *Ibid.*, p. 24.
5. Ian Jack, *The Augustan Satire* (London: OUP, 1956), p. 78.
6. *Ibid.*, p. 82.
7. *Ibid.*, pp. 93-94.
8. *Ibid.*, pp. 94-95.

6

An Epistle to Dr Arbuthnot

An Epistle to Dr Arbuthnot followed *An Essay on Man* and, in many senses, this poem represents Pope's view of life. No doubt, there is satire but it is not entirely negative. The people who have gone against Pope's ideals are satirised critically and bitterly and the people who fit in the framework of his ideals are dealt with tenderness.

An Epistle to Dr Arbuthnot is an autobiographical poem and most of the characters are drawn from real life. Besides, they are not fictionalised; they are portrayed as Pope understood and estimated them. The first character, is, of course, Dr. John Arbuthnot, M.D. (1667-1735), who was a leading practitioner of Pope's time. Queen Anne had appointed him Physician-in-Ordinary to her. He worked at St. Andrew's Hospital and wrote many learned books on medicine. Besides, he was a man of fine literary taste and wrote *Memoirs of Martinus Scriblerus* and *History of John Bull*. Later on, John Bull became the symbol of England. He was Pope's best friend.

According to John Butt, Pope's greatest editor, *An Epistle to Dr Arbuthnot* was written on the doctor's request to continue "his [Pope's] tirade against vice. The poem was written in piecemeal over two or three years. Unfortunately, Dr. Arbuthnot died soon (1735). Pope was in a hurry to get it published when he found that his dearest friend was seriously ill. He, therefore, got the poem published separately. *The Collected Works* was published later. The idea was that his friend could see that his friend had complied with his request and also that he could read the poem in its printed form.

The poem is in the style of Horace. It is in the form of dialogue where P is Pope and A is Arbuthnot. It begins dramatically:

Shut, shut the door, good John: fatigued, I said;
Tie up the knocker, say I'm sick, I'm dead.
The Dog-star rages! nay 'tis past a doubt,
All bedlam, or Parnassus, is let out
Fire in each eye, and papers in each hand,
They rave, recite, and madden round the land. (1-6)

Apart from his anger expressed against his literary adversaries, these lines, and the entire poem, are a great technical achievement of Pope. In poems like *Essay on Criticism*, *The Rape of the Lock* and *An Essay on Man*, he has a persona to observe on the events of the world. Here, he has thrown down the persona and got himself in the tangle; he is both actor and observer. Secondly, he has discarded the urbanity and formality of poetic diction. All the quoted lines, maintaining stateliness, are prosaic, conversational and expressive of personal anguish. The people whom he does not want to enter his room are Joseph Addison, Colley Cibber, Ambrose Philips, John Dennis, Richard Bentley and Baron Hervey.

Dog-star is Cirius, the brightest star in the sky. But its appearance is not liked by people as it brings dog-days, the summer of extreme heat. It also indicates the turning of people's heads. In other words, it heralds the days of madness. Then Pope calls the people coming to him as mad and poetasters. He feels deeply distressed at their mad behaviour and says that he is plagued by them day and night. There is no respite for him.

No place is sacred, nor the Church is free,
Even Sunday shines no Sabbath—day to me:
Then from the Mint Walks for the man of rhyme.
Happy! to catch me, just at dinner-time. (11-14)

Pope's wit sparkles in the last line of the quoted passage. In our time people phone at lunch and dinner time. In those days people called at lunch or dinner time because they were sure that the desired man would be at home. After ridiculing his pursuers, he counts the people who disturb him. The first is Arthur Moore whose son James plagiarised six of Pope's lines. He is also ridiculed in *The Dunciad*:

> Arthur, whose giddy son neglects the laws,
> Imputes to me and my damned works the cause:
> Poor Cornus sees his frantic wife elope,
> And curses wit, and poetry, and Pope. (23-26)

The next person is an unworthy poet here called Pitholeon a stupid poet in Horace's *Satires*, who pesters him off and on.

> Pitholeon sends to me: "You know his grace,
> I want a patron; ask him for a place."
> 'Pitholeon libelled me'—But here's a letter
> Informs you, Sir, 't was when he knew no better.
> (49-52)

Then comes Curll, the notorious publisher who had tricked Pope:

> ...Curll invites me to dine,
> He'll write a journal, or he'll turn divine.
> Bless me! a packet, 'Tis a stranger sues,
> A virgin tragedy, an orphan Muse;
> If I dislike it, "Furies, death and rage!"
> If I approve, "Commend it to the stage."

If the unknown poet, named Pitholeon here, and Curll, the publisher, have cheated him, Lintot who published Pope for fourteen years, too, had not been honest to him:

> "Lintot, dull rogue! will think your price too much:"
> "Not, Sir, if you revise it, and retouch."
> All my demurs but double his attacks;
> At last he whispers, "Do, and we go snacks."
> Glad of a quarrel, straight I clap the door:
> Sir, let me see your works and you no more. (62-67)

Pope laments his awkward situation. He is asked by publishers to go through the poems by inferior poets and praise them profusely which he cannot do because their faults are as large as the ears of King Midas. It is the myth that King Midas' ears grew as large as those of a donkey. When Pope compares the faults of the poets with those of Midas' ears, he indirectly means that the faulty poets are asses.

Arbuthnot tries to pacify him and plays pun with King Midas' story:

> Good friend, forbear! you deal in dangerous things,
> I'd never name queens, ministers, or kings:
> Keep close to ears and those let asses prick,
> 'tis nothing.... (75-78)

But Pope is not satisfied. He reacts:

> Nothing? if they bite and kick?
> Out with it, Dunciad! let the secret pass,
> That secret to each fool, that he's an ass:
> The truth once told (and wherefore should we lie?)
> The queen of Midas slept, and so may I.... (79-83)

Then he enumerates the wrong-doers and the wrongs done to him. The first is Codrus, a poet ridiculed by Juvenal and here Elkanah Settle. He calls him a fool and a spider. After him are Colley and Henley and the Freemason Moore. Arbuthnot asks him not to name the people. It is too much and after all Colley Cibber is the poet Laureate. But Pope continues his tirade and says that they are all hypocrites. They say one thing and do another:

> One dedicates in high heroic prose,
> And ridicules beyond a hundred foes:
> One from all Grub Street will my name defend,
> And, more abusive, calls himself my friend
> This prints my letters, that expects a bribe,
> And others roar aloud, "Subscribe, subscribe". (109-14)

This initial outburst of anger shows Pope's sensitivity. In fact, he had a vision of life which he outlined in *An Essay on Man.* Dustin H. Griffin remarks:

> In them, we can see more clearly than anywhere else in Pope's poetry that his own sensibility stands at the base of

> his poetic world and is, paradoxically, a means for Pope to encompass a wider world. Study of his own character and experience provides him a focus for exploring the kinds of moral and psychological demands and predicaments that confront all those who, like himself, must live in a world at once exhilarating, gratifying, and offensive.[1]

The dramatic form of the poem, like other Horatian imitations, has its important characteristic. The conversation is between Pope and his friend, Dr. Arbuthnot. Thomas Edwards has pointed out that the two persons in the poem are two selves of Pope. Arbuthnot is the more rational and discreet self. He is worldly side of Pope, the skilful man of business, the prudent, calculating man who won for a disabled poet (Pope himself said that he appeared like a spider, short body, long hands and legs), not only the recognition of the world but also a full measure of its rewards. The rewards were wealth, material comfort, rich and powerful friends and the very liberty to speak out in opposition.

Griffin rightly says:

> The *Epistle* is a personal drama in which Pope attempts to work out and present in verse some of the conflicts within himself or between his various selves—good man, professional poet, son and friend, defender of virtue, lover of peace, irritable war faring wit.[2]

Lines 135 onwards give us a good idea of Pope's different selves and his view of life. First, he tells us who his true friends are. He counts the names of his friends like Lord Lansdowne Granville (poet and statesman), William Walsh (poet and a Whig), Sir Samuel Garth (poet and director), Jonathan Swift, Duke of Shrewsbury (Talbot), Baron Somers (a Whig and Lord Chancellor), Duke of Buckingham, Viscount Bolingbroke, William Congreve, Henry St. John and Bishop Francis Attenbury. They are praised in glowing words:

> But why then publish? Granville the polite,
> And knowing Walsh, would tell me I could write;
> Well-natured Garth inflamed with early praise,
> And Congreve loved and Swift endured my lays;

The courtly Talbot, Somers, Shefield read,
Even mitred Rochester would not the head,
And St. John's self (great Dryden's friend before)
With open arms received one poet more. (135-42)

For Pope these people are great lovers of poetry and are generous at heart. They are in contrast to Lintot, Curll and Cibber who pay no attention to good poetry and, also, cheat innocent poets like Pope:

Happy my studies, when by these approved!
Happier their author, when by these beloved!
From these the world will judge of men and books,
Not from the Burnets, Oldmixons, and Cookes.
(143-46)

It is a well-known fact that Burnet and Oldmixon, both historians and Cooke, a minor poet, criticised Pope's poetry. Pope continues to say that he wrote poetry offending none. In fairness to him it can be said that his early poems—*The Pastorals, Essay on Criticism, The Rape of the Lock* and *An Essay on Man*—did not satirise anyone. The poems do not make any kind of attack on any man of his time. He is right and fully justified when he says:

Soft were my numbers; who could take offence
While pure description, held the place of sense?
Like gentle Fanny's was my flowery theme,
A painted mistress, or a purling stream. (147-50)

Ill-natured people like Charles Gildon and John Dennis badly criticised his immortal poems. Wrongly, yet he never replied, though he knew them to be madcaps or paid agents. He always remained calm and quiet. He humbly bowed to those who praised him and smiled gently if someone pointed defects in his poetry.

Then he pardons them all his adversaries and says:

Peace to all such.

However, he finds it difficult to forget the injustice done to him by Joseph Addison, here named Atticus. Joseph Addison was a stalwart among the men of letters in the eighteenth century. An influential M.P. and man of large fortune, he patronized the young creative writers. His *Spectator* was the leading periodical. As a young poet Pope went to him regularly but he found that his attitude was too patronizing and also that he was a big snob. Anthony Trott gives three reasons for Pope's attack on Addison:

1. Addison's patronising attitude to young poets (including Pope) was not liked by Pope.
2. Addison did not praise and support Pope's translation. of the *Iliad*; worse still Addison praised the performance of a rival translator; and Pope had pinned his hopes on his work.
3. Addison's earlier advice not to include the Machinery of Spirits in *The Rape of the Lock*—when the poem gained by the inclusion of it—still rankled in Pope's heart.[3]

Pope draws a picture of Addison. For him, Addison is a diffident person. He can never praise a person whole-heartedly nor denounce the other in plain words. In other words, nobody can say who his friend is and who is his enemy; he offends both in turns. Pope expresses his anguish at Addison's strange behaviour as he never expected him to be such a hypocrite. He writes about him:

> ...but were there one whose fires
> True genius kindles, and fair fame inspires;
> Blest with each talent, and each art to please,
> And born to write, converse, and live with ease;
> Should such a man, too fond to rule alone.
> Bear, like the Turk, no brother near the throne,
> View him with scornful, yet with jealous eyes,
> And hate for arts that caused him to rise. (193-200)

Having criticised Addison for his lack of literary taste, Pope attacks him for his wavering mind and hypocritical behaviour. In his opinion Addison is inherently a weak man who:

> Is willing to wound, and yet afraid to strike,
> Just hint a fault, and hestitate dislike

Alike reserved to blame, or to commend,
A timorous foe, and a suspicious friend;
Dreading even fools, by flatterers besieged,
And so obliging, that he never obliged. (203-08)

Griffin considers, Joseph Addison, here Atticus, to be the antiself of Pope. He explains his viewpoint:

> More important than the adversarius in Pope's process of self-definition, however, is a figure we might call the adversary. Seen especially in *Arbuthnot*, but occurring in other poems as well, this figure—Atticus, Sporus, Walpole, Cibber—is primarily designed as Pope's antithesis, an antiself and thereby an aid to self-definition. For Pope's sense of himself seems to have been strengthened and clarified by the presence of a real or imagined other against which he himself might thrust. He seems most articulate, most himself, when he finds or places himself in opposition, whether in the personal literary quarrels that occupied most of his adult life, the political opposition to Walpole in the 1730s, or the eleborate poetic fantasies in which an embattled Pope faces a world of vicious enemies.
>
> But the effectiveness of the contrast between Pope and his antiselves may well depend on the striking resemblances each figure bears to Pope in a number of particulars. Consider first the portrait of Atticus in the *Epistle to Arbuthnot*.[4]

After this, he quotes lines 193-214 of the poem.

It is very difficult to disagree with a great scholar like Griffin I agree with every word he has said but find it rather difficult to take Atticus as Pope's antiself. In my opinion Addison is a kind of man whom Pope considered a big snob, a *poseur* who behaved like a monarch of poets. Addison is a person who is in sharp contrast with Pope. He is first of all a distinctly pointed version of all that Pope dislikes. He is by and large a jealous, timorous, suspicious and self-aggrandizing man. Atticus's deceptive civility makes a clear contrast with Pope's manner as friend and as critic. These lines expose Addison's character:

Like Cato, give his little Senate laws,
And sit attentive to his own applause;
While wits and templars every sentence raise,
And wonder with a foolish face of praise
Who but must laugh, if such a man there be?
Who would not weep, if Atticus were he? (209-14)

This passage and the previously quoted passages make Pope's attitude to Addison clear. When Pope, the critic, praises his friends Dr. Arbuthnot and John Gay, famous writer of *The Beggar's Opera*, or his beloved parents he does so openly and fully. When he blames, it is not by "faint praise" or by hinting or hesitating. He speaks out plainly and boldly. Indeed, the outspoken manner he adopts in the poem derives in part from his wish to put as much distance as possible between himself and Addison. Here I agree with Griffin when he comments:

> Where Pope places deep value on friendship, declares himself a fearless friend of virtue, and does not hesitate to strike with his lash against his foes, Atticus is a timorous foe and a suspicious friend.[5]

Cato and his little senate also form an apt contrast to Pope amidst his literary circle. Atticus is a jealous ruler who is intolerant of all his equals. He conducts sessions of his little senate not to pronounce clearly on the merits and faults of contemporary writers or to encourage and promote excellence. On the contrary, he likes to receive the applause of the foolish "Wits and templars" who flatter him. His laws and sentences are handed down only in order that the lawgiver's own wit may be praised. For his part, too, Pope receives the praise of a literary circle. He is not a dictator but an apprentice.

The circle Pope joins is of course a distinguished one while Atticus's is made up of fools and flatterers. Pope's friends are all equal but Addison's are inferiors. Pope has a vivid sense of confraternity and of the heritage of merit. As a poet he joins a tradition. But Atticus gains a petty throne. The most important difference, however, lies in the interrelations of the literary circle. Pope's literary happiness comes through the approval and the love of his fellow poets.

Even when Pope has later gained literary prominence, he refuses to act the dictator. He reluctantly hears the appeals of the flattering poetasters, dismisses them politely when they become tiresome:

> What though my name stood rubric on the walls,
> Or plastered posts, with claps, in capitals?
> Or smoking forth, a hundred hawkers load,
> On wings of winds came flying all abroad?
> I sought no homage from the race that write. (215-19)

A little later, he writes:

> I never with wits or witlings passed my days
> To spread about the itch of verse and praise;
> Nor like a puppy, daggled through the town,
> To fetch and carry, sing-song up and down. (225-28)

In a position to help a writer in need, Pope does not hesitate to aid even his enemies:

> This dreaded satirist Dennis will confess
> Foe to his pride, but friend to his distress
> So humble, he has knocked at Tibbald's door
> Has drunk with Cibber, nay has rhymed for Moor.
> (370-73)

The differences between Pope and Addison are especially significant because they exist within a ground of similarity. Both were in their times literary figures of great power, in positions to influence the cultural and moral life of the nation. However, Addison, being senior and socially more respected, wielded greater influence. In fairness to him, it can be said that he gave a new direction to English prose through *The Spectator* in general and his own essays in particular. This is why Pope is a bit diffident in *An Epistle to Dr Arbuthnot* in pointing out the major differences. He is rather more anxious to convince his readers of the clear distinction between him and Addison. Hence, he takes some risks in describing Addison (Atticus) in terms that may recall his own case. Griffin comments:

> That Pope was at least covertly aware of the similarity is suggested by some parallels in phrasing and in ideas on

lesser points. Atticus was "born to write...and live with ease". Pope too, was "dipped in ink" at birth and "lisped in numbers, for the numbers came" (that is, with ease) and he claims that he has little business else than to "Maintain a Poet's Dignity and Ease".[6]

The next person under Pope's attack is Sporus, Baron Hervey in real life. Pope has changed Spodrus to Sporus but the meaning is quite clear.

Like Atticus, Sporus is the prime target of Pope's attack. According to Griffin, his character is designed primarily to set off Pope's own manly virtue and serves, at times, as a covert self-parody. Whether he is a parody of Pope's self or not but it is certain that Lord Hervey's weaknesses are ridiculously exposed:

Let Sporus tremble—What that thing of silk,
Sporus, that mere white curd of asses' milk,
Satire or sense, alas! can Sporus feel?
Who breaks a butterfly upon a wheel
Yet let me flap this bug with gilded wings,
This painted child of dirt, that stinks and stings
Whose buzz the witty and the fair annoys
Yet wit never tastes, and beauty never enjoys
So well-bred Spaniels civilly delight
In mumbling of the game they dare not bite. (305-14)

Here Lord Hervey is portrayed as a timid fellow. He is compared to a piece of cloth made of silk which trembles at a light wind. He is curd of ass's milk. The curd of a cow is thick and hard but of an ass is thin and soft and is given to babies. Though he is delicate in body, he is insensitive to satire or a serious idea. His strength lies in breaking a butterfly on a wheel. He is past appreciating beauty and wit. Finally, he is like a spaniel dog, too small to bite anyone. The satire continues:

Eternal smiles his emptiness betray
As shallow streams run dimpling all the way.
Whether in florid impotence he speaks
And as the prompter breathes, the puppet squeaks

Or at the ear of Eve, familiar toad
Half froth, half venom, spits himself abroad
In puns, or politics, or tales or lies
Or spite, or smut, or rhymes, or blasphemies. (45-52)

It is clearly a portrait of John Hervey. As John Butt and Maynard Mack, both editors of Pope's works, have pointed out, some of the details in Pope's attack derive from earlier printed attack on Hervey, most prominently William Puteney's *Proper Reply to a Late Scurrilous Libel* (1731), where Hervey is described as a "circulator of tittle-tattle, a bearer of tales, a teller of fibs, a stationed spy". He is sexually ambiguous: "You know that he is a lady himself; or at least such a nice composition of the two sexes, that it is difficult to distinguish which is most predominant...a delicate Hermaphrodite such a pretty, little, master-miss." His wit is laborious yet vapid: "the little, quaint antitheses, the laboured Gingle of the Periods, the great variety of rhetorical flourishes, affected metaphors, and puerile witticisms".[7]

Similar attacks were made by other writers also. In fact, attacks and counterattacks were quite common in the eighteenth century and most of the writers concealed their names. In all attacks, a favourite target was Hervey's affected effeminate manner and his lady-like beautiful but painted face.

Lord Hervey's sexual ambiguity is further derided:

Amphibious thing! that acting either part
The trifling head, or the corrupted heart!
Fop at the toilet, flatterer at the board
Now trips a lady, and now struts a lord
Eve's tempter thus, the rabbins have expressed
A cherub face, a reptile all the race. (336-41)

This portrait of Sporus (Lord Hervey) is based on the facts known to the people. Pope has not crossed the limits of decency because such things were printed earlier in pamphlets and books.

The next person criticized is John Dennis. Pope has sufficient reason to satirize him. Much earlier before the writing of the

Epistle, John Dennis had portrayed Pope as a Satan with an angel face in *True Character* (1716). He wrote in *Pamphlet* about Pope:

> By his constant and malicious lying, and by that angel face and form of his, it is plain that he wants nothing but horns and tail, to be the exact resemblance, both in shape and mind, of his Infernal Father.

Truly, the main thrust of the pamphlet was to deride Pope's frail body and health. This verse, quoted by Griffin, attacks Pope in the form of instructions to a sculptor:

> There carve a pert, but yet a rueful face
> Half man, half monkey, owned by neither race.
> This his mis-shapen form: but say what art
> Can frame the monstrous image of his heart.
> Composed of malice, envy, discontent,
> Like his limbs crooked, like them impotent.[8]

Pope replied in a mild way in the Epistle:

> There are, who to my person pay their court:
> I cough like Horace, and, though lean, am short.
> Ammon's great son one shoulder had too high—
> Such Ovid's nose,—and, "Sir! you have an eye".
> Go on obliging creatures, make me see
> All that disgraced my betters met in me
> Say, for my comfort, languishing in bed,
> Just so immortal Maro held his head;
> And when I die, be sure you let me know
> Great Homer died three thousand years ago. (116-25)

He reminds Dennis of his benevolence done to the latter and his group in the past:

> This dreaded satirist Dennis will confess.
> Foe to his pride, but friend to his distress:
> So humble, he has knocked at Tibbald's door,
> Has drunk with Cibber, nay has rhymed for Moore.
> (370-73)

As already said, the younger Moore had plagiarised lines from Pope's poetry and Colley Cibber had become Poet Laureate by influencing the Crown. Pope is pained that the person whom he helped in the past has started criticising him and associating with mean fellows like Moore and Cibber. Credit should be given to him that he has not used scurrilous words for Dennis. Perhaps, the reason for his restrain is that he knew that big people like Lord Hervey and Joseph Addison were behind them.

The other person associated with Dennis is Charles Gildon who harshly criticised Pope's poems. Here Pope says that in spite of their venomous criticism, he has remained rather stoic.

> Yet then did Gildon draw his venal quill;
> I wished the man a dinner and sate still.
> Yet then did Dennis rave in furious fret;
> I never answered—I was not in debt.
> If want provoked, or madness made them print,
> I waged no war with Bedlam or the Mint. (151-56)

Pope ends his defence by satirising his adversaries, chiefly publishers and bad critics:

> Let Budgell charge low Grub Street on his quill.
> And write whatever he pleased, except his will;
> Let the two Curlls of town and court abuse.
> His father, mother, body, soul, and Muse,
> Yet why? that father held it for a rule,
> It was a sin to call our neighbour a fool:
> That harmless mother thought no wife a whore
> Hear this, and spare his family, James Moore! (379-86)

Against this quarrelsome and howling public life, there is Pope's private life, a life made rich by the support and love of his parents and friends. He remembers his parents:

> Of gentle blood (part shed in honour's cause,)
> While yet in Britain honour had applause
> Each parent sprung—A. What fortune,
> pray? Their own
> And better got, than Bestia's from the throne

Born to no pride, inheriting no strife,
Nor marrying discord in a noble wife.
Stranger to civil and religious rage,
The good man walked innoxious through his age.
(388-95)

The first three lines tell us about his parentage that he comes from a good family "of gentle blood". In other words, his forefathers were neither serf nor peasant. Secondly, he is a true British, not an emigrant. When Arbuthnot asks, "What fortune, pray", Pope answers: "their own". It will be relevant to add that Pope's father was a linen merchant who carried on business on Lombard Street. This was a street where most of the banks flourished. Trade was not considered a noble profession in the medieval period but it began to gain importance during Chaucer's time and the middle class became important in the seventeenth century. After the Glorious Revolution, the middle class began to hold the sway and the House of Commons became as powerful as the House of Lords.

Pope's father gathered money in due course. After amassing wealth he retired from business and bought a country house, near Windsor Forest at Brinfield. Nearness to the Windsor Forest had an exhilarating effect on Pope. He developed a natural piety with the country scene and a calm, sedate life, far from the madding crowd. His first poem written at the age of twelve, "Ode on Solitude", is an expression of Pope's view of ideal life. The idea that he expressed in his known earliest poem again finds the place in the *Epistle*. Lines 391-95 of the previously quoted passage describe the happy life his father and mother led. Pope says that his father was a trader but a very honest man. He was unlike Bestia, the Roman ambassador who went over to the enemy side on being given a bribe. In other words, he did not accept dowry which was a system in the seventeenth century. The aristocratic people accepted dowry and fought bitterly for inheritance. The poet says that as his father was honest to the core and earned money by honest means, he was free from all kinds of disputes and quarrels. He was humble and benign, and so, there was never a discord between him and his wife. He was never involved in civil and religious disputes. He was a good man and lived a true, happy and innocuous life.

It will be pertinent to add here the important events in Pope's life for a better understanding of *An Epistle to Dr Arbuthnot* which is basically autobiographical.

Pope was born on 21 May 1688, the year of the Glorious Revolution and the demise of Catholic ascendancy. As his father was a catholic, the air he inhaled was not of peace and beatitude but of hostility. Being the son of a Catholic he was not allowed to be admitted to a public school and so could not get the opportunity to receive education formally. He taught himself to write by copying print. This great labour of copying printed letters made his handwriting one of the finest in the literary circle in his mature life. Throughout his life his fine and graceful handwriting reminded people of his hard practice.

He received his early education from a priest. His father had given shelter to this priest in his own house, and the grateful priest repaid the kindness by teaching the young boy the rudiments of Latin and Greek. Later, young Pope was sent to two schools by turn, but both of them being Catholic were of a very bad state. His school days were practically over by the time he reached the twelfth year and then began his attempt at self-education. He took to reading by himself with great eagerness and enthusiasm. He had a special penchant for poetry. He read the Greek and Latin classics in translation and as the vogue in those days was he aspired to be a great poet.

Pope was not a healthy child. He was short in size. His growth was retarded by a severe illness. He could not reach the height of even five feet. He was a dwarf by the British standard. He remained deformed, in spite of his sharp features, throughout his life. The short size and the mis-shapen body precluded him from the possibility of embracing any active profession. Besides, he had to look after his health with constant care for the preservation of life. Later on, his critics, especially Dennis derided his deformed body. Griffin refers to the poem *Verses Addressed to the Imitator of Horace* where Pope is described as both wasp and reptile and quotes the following passage where he is called a splenetic toad:

The stinking venom flows around,
And nauseous slaver hides the ground.
Yet not one mortal, whom it hit
'T was just as harmless as his wit.
For take away the filthy part
Of T-d, and spew, and mud, and fart.

Elsewhere he is a Spaniel:

And ever after, 't was their drift
A spaniel P-pe a mastiff Sw-t.

As Jonathan Swift was of standard height he is called a mastiff and the short-size Pope, a spaniel.

Pope suffered practically throughout his life from illness. Headache always pestered him. It was natural that he suffered from a kind of nervous irritability. An undercurrent of unhappiness pricked him all through because he was deprived of many things as a youth he could enjoy. The only solace, then for him was studying books and writing poetry. These lines in the *Epistle* are the result of his agony.

Why did I write? What sin to me unknown
Dipt me in my ink—my parents' or my own?
As yet a child, nor yet a fool to fame,
I lisped in numbers, for the numbers came,
I left no calling for this idle trade
No duty broke, no father disobeyed:
The Muse but served to ease some friend, not wife
To help me through this long disease, my life.[9] (125-32)

Later on, asthma and dropsy made his life more miserable. This is one of the reasons why he never married.

Thus, Pope always lived in tension. On one side was his aspiration to live a calm and quiet life in solitude and on the other was the long illness that deprived him of all pleasures of life. The only solace for him was poetry but critics like Addison, Dennis and Lord Hervey made his career a hell and tricksters like James Moore and Colly Cibber cheated him. In this situation, he got support from his friends like John Gay, William Walsh,

Dr. Arbuthnot, Jonathan Swift, Sir Samuel Garth, Sir Trumbull and a few more. They are named in the *Epistle*.

The first and foremost is Dr. Arbuthnot who supported Pope when he was attacked by critics and saved his life whenever he fell seriously ill. He expresses his gratitude in these lines:

Friend to my life! (Which did not you prolong,
The world had wanted many an idle song)
What drop or nostrum can this plague remove? (27-29)

He further says in lines 133-34:

To second, Arbuthnot! thy art and care,
And teach the being you preserved to bear.

Towards the end of the poem, he remembers the service the doctor did to his ailing mother. The tribute he pays is quite rich. At first, he wishes him good health and peace of mind:

O Friend! may each domestic bliss be thine
Be no unpleasing melancholy mine. (406-07)

Then he recollects how the doctor saved his ailing mother's life:

Me, let the tender office long engage.
To rock the cradle of reposing age,
With lenient arts extend a mother's breath
Make languor smile, and smooth the bed of death.
Explore the thought, explain the asking eye.
And keep awhile one parent from the sky. (408-13)

Finally, he wishes him a happy and prosperous life:

May heaven, to bless those days, preserve my friend,
Preserve him social, cheerful, and serene
And just as rich as when he served a queen. (415-17)

He thanks his friends who helped him positively in his efforts to build his poetical career;

But why then publish? Granville the polite,
And knowing Walsh, would tell me I could write,
Well-natured Garth inflamed with early praise,
And Congreve loved, and Swift endured my lays;

> The courtly Talbot, Somers, Sheffield read
> Even mitred Rochester would nod the head
> And St. John's self (great, Dryden's friend before)
> With open arms received one poet more
> Happy my studies, when by these approved! (135-43)

According to Griffin:

> *Epistle to Dr Arbuthnot* dramatizes the conflict between Pope as defender of virtue, sallying forth into a world of knaves to lash the vicious and rescue Truth in distress and Pope as contemplative recluse, shrinking from contact with the loud, impudent importunate world, seeking the consolations of quiet, books, friendship and family.[10]

But a little later, he observes that Pope fails to arrive at a happy reconciliation and the public and private lives remain at war. Here is the remark:

> In *Arbuthnot* the conflicting claims of the private life and of a larger world are finally unreconciled.[11]

He gives a long argument to prove his point of view. But I feel that his observation is not correct. Thomas Edwards, an eminent American critic whom he refutes writes in *This Dark Estate* (pp. 105-06):

> The poem [*Epistle to Dr Arbuthnot*] is a masterpiece of modulation, a 'rising and falling of emotion, from equanimity to violence and back again'.

The same idea has been expressed by Elias Mengel in his article "Patterns of Imagery in Pope's *Arbuthnot*", PMLA, 69 (1954), 189 that Pope harassed and plagued by fools and knaves, patient and enduringly tolerant until he can no longer hold back explosive anger, lashes out at his critics and again recovers a measure of calm.

Professor G. Wilson Knight also holds the view that Pope achieves equanimity in *Arbuthnot*. He writes:

> This epistle shows a blend of violence and gentleness, varying between attack and pathos, social criticism and autobiography, swelling and subsiding with an undulatory movement whose balance repays attention. His chief

boasts, of looking after his mother to the last and cherishing a deep friendship, are not those of a misanthrope: he is never submerged by his satire, but well above it.[12]

In other words, he achieves equanimity. Generally, a poem's concluding lines express its author's intention. *An Epistle to Dr Arbuthnot* is a long poem and so, its last fifty lines or so express Pope's intention in writing it. A close analysis of the poem presents the real portrait of the poet. The total picture is this. A physically weak but mentally alert young poet strives to achieve greatness. In real life he finds the world hostile to him. Being a Catholic he is denied the basic human rights. Later on, Joseph Addison, the leading man of letters of the time, does not encourage him as he should. He proves to be a big snob. The critics deride him and publishers cheat him. It is too much for a poet who is more sensitive than an average man. He finds solace in the company of friends who are really talented. Walsh, Gay, Swift, Congreve and Arbuthnot are prominent among them. Apart from these there are Viscount Bolingbroke, Lord Trumbull and other lords and ladies. The balance between the bad people and the good people tilts towards the latter. The poet gains equanimity:

Oh let me live my own, and die so too!
(To live and die is all I have to do:)
Maintain a poet's dignity and ease
And see what friends, and read what
books and please. (361-64)

Finally, he remembers his father's calm but dignified life:

No courts he saw, no suits would ever try,
Nor dared on oath, nor hazarded a lie.
Unlearned, he knew no schoolman's subtle art,
No language, but the language of the heart.
By nature honest, by experience wise,
Healthy by Temperance, and by exercise,
His life, though long, to sickness passed unknown
His death was instant, and without a groan. (396-403)

Pope, too, wishes this kind of life, he prays to God:

O grant me thus to live, and thus to die. (404)

An Epistle to Dr Arbuthnot can be said to be Pope's testament. Here he has been able to combine nature, art and man successfully, all following the Higher Order.

Notes

1. Dustin H. Griffin, *Studies in Pope's Poetry*, p. 165.
2. *Ibid*., p. 168.
3. Anthony Trott and Martin Axford, ed., "Introduction". *The Epistles and Satires of Alexander Pope* (London: Macmillan, 1975), p. viii.
4. Dustin H. Griffin, *op. cit*., p. 173.
5. *Ibid*., p. 174.
6. *Ibid*., p. 176.
7. John Butt ed., "Notes", *Works of Pope* (Oxford: OUP, 1960), p. 710.
8. Quoted by Dustin H. Griffin, *Studies in Pope's Poetry*, p. 185.
9. *Ibid*., pp. 184-85.
10. *Ibid*., p. 198.
11. *Ibid*., p. 200.
12. G. Wilson Knight, *Laureate of Peace*, pp. 69-70.

7

The Dunciad

The Dunciad was first published in 1728. At that time, it contained three Books. Later on, Pope revised it and added the fourth Book and called it *The New Dunciad*. The 1743 edition is called *The Dunciad*. This poem complex in technique is like *An Epistle to Dr Arbuthnot* autobiographical.

The people satirised are Theobald and Cibber. Lewis Theobald was a scholar of Shakespeare and playwright. Pope's 1725 edition of Shakespeare provoked him to publish *Shakespeare Restored* in 1726. He incorporated a few of the emendations made by Pope. But this debt did not pacify Pope and he satirized him in *Peri Bathous* and made him the hero of the first book of *The Dunciad*.

Colley Cibber, as already mentioned in the previous chapter was a playwright and poet. He was appointed Poet Laureate in 1730. As he did not belong to Pope's party, he became one of his adversaries and was made the king of dunces in the remaining three Books of *The Dunciad*.

Commenting on the development of *The Dunciad* from three Books to four Books, Ian Jack says:

> There is no doubt that the model of the poem as it was then published (in 1728) was *Mac Flecknoe*. Like Dryden's poem the *Dunciad* of 1728 describes the succession of one dunce to another on the throne of Dullness. The general

resemblance is particularly evident in Book I, at the opening of Book II, and in the design of Book III.

Yet it is clear that Pope's object is not identical with Dryden's—attack on a personal enemy by means of ridicule. For after the description of Theobald simpering self-consciously on an immense throne in the opening lines he is a mere spectator for the rest of Book II, which is devoted to the "high heroic games" in which booksellers and other bad writers celebrate his coronation. It is clear that Pope wished to satirize not only Theobald but a host of bad writers, ignorant patrons, and unscrupulous publishers.[1]

The second target of Pope's satire is the levelling down of literary standards. Martinus Scriblerus remarks in his Preface:

> He lived in those days, when (after providence had permitted the Invention of Printing as a scourge for the sins of the learned) paper also became so cheap, and printers so numerous, that a deluge of authors covered the land: whereby not only the peace of the honest unwriting subject was daily molested, but unmerciful demands were made of his applause, yea of his money, by such as would neither earn the one, or deserve the other: at the same time the liberty of the press was so unlimited that it grew dangerous to refuse them either. Our author did conceive it an endeavour well worthy of an honest satirist, to dissuade the dull and punish the malicious, the only way that was left. In that public-spirited view he laid the plan of this poem.

A little later he writes that the "action of the *Dunciad* is the removal of the imperial seat of dullness from the city to the polite world".

It may be asked: Who is Martinus Scriblerus? The answer is that he is a fictitious person. The name is not English. The reality is that a group of Tory intellectuals and writers formed a club and named it The Scriblerus Club in 1713. Its purpose was to discuss topics of contemporary interests and ridicule "all the false tastes of learning. The members were Pope, Swift, Arbuthnot, Gay, Parnell, Atterbury, Congreve and Robert Harley.

Collectively, they invented Martinus Scriblerus, a pedantic hack who would write on all serious topics."[2]

It is certain then the Preface was written by Pope himself and his friends helped him in giving its final shape. Thus, *The Dunciad*, in the words of Ian Jack,

> is not only an attack on bad writers and bad writing: it is Pope's pessimistic commentary on an important development of civilization of his time. It is a bitter protest against the levelling down of literary standards.[3]

The four books describe the triumph of Dullness. In Book I Bayes (Colley Cibber) is anointed Poet Laureate on the death of Eusden. Book II describes the celebrations following Bayes' enthronement as King of the Dunces, presiding over the empire of Emptiness and Dullness. The celebrations are a burlesque of the funeral games for Anchises in the *Aeneid*. Everyone falls asleep while poetry is being read. In Book III Bayes sees in his dreams the past and future triumphs of the empire of Dullness extended to all arts and sciences, the theatre, and the court. His guide is Settle, one of Dryden's opponents. Book IV sees the dream realized, thought is discouraged and Dullness triumphs in a final vision of cultural chaos, part comic and part serious.

The Dunciad in its revised form may be called Pope's last major work. Pope right from the beginning of his career felt that his contemporaries were not following the principle of correctness so meticulously practised by John Dryden. He, therefore, advised his contemporaries to follow nature in *Essay on Criticism* and *An Essay on Man*. A.L. Williams in his scholarly study of *The Dunciad* gives the reason why Pope criticised the deviators and called them Dunce:

> The age was a time of great and profound changes, changes which many could only view, though perhaps mistakenly, with deep pessimism. Scientific and philosophical developments of the seventeenth century were effecting radical modifications in the old attitudes and values. At the same time the traditional social and political structures were feeling the strain caused by the growth of a large

> and powerful middle class. The tastes of a broad new class of readers, barely literate by Pope's standards, were being satisfied, and pandered to, by writers who appeared to many to be, if not totally ignorant of a great literary tradition, at least irresponsible in their obligations toward that tradition. In addition, there was the effect wrought on the literary scene by the release of a race of hired political writers, some of whom could be persuaded, as Defoe was, to write for both the Whigs and the Tories simultaneously. As Pope points out in one of his notes to the *Dunciad* it was estimated by a committee appointed to investigate Walpole's administration that no less than fifty-thousand, seventy-seven pounds, eighteen shillings, were paid to authors and printers of newspapers such as Free Britons, Daily-Courants, Corn-Cutter's Journals, Gazetteers, and other political papers, between Feb. 10, 1731 and Feb. 10, 1741.[4]

The political situation and the role of money-minded writers and periodicals made the right thinking and honest people gloomy. Pope and many of his contemporaries seriously felt that cultural doom was looming at large. Besides, inferior writers borrowed indiscriminately from the classical writers. The result was inappropriate borrowings and applications, mean imitations and vulgar paraphrases. It is against this background that *The Dunciad* was written. Although written at different times, it has a kind of continuity which can be traced when we look at Pope's life. As we have already read *An Epistle to Dr Arbuthnot*, Pope was provoked by his critics and mean publishers. The people whom he criticised in the *Epistle* are also attacked in *The Dunciad* with a greater force. Like *The Rape of the Lock*, *The Dunciad* is also written in the style of an epic partly. The opening lines remind us of Virgil's *Aeneid* and Milton's *Paradise Lost*:

> Books and the Man I sing, the first who brings
> The Smithfield Muses to the Ear of Kings.
> Say great Patrician! (since your selves inspire
> These Wonderous works; so Jove and Fate require)

Say from what cause, in vain decryed and curst,
Still Dunce the second reigns like Dunce the first.

(I, 1-6)

The Aeneid begins thus:

Of arms and man I sing, the first which brings.

The reference to Smithfield in the opening lines is significant. The king and the nobility began to patronize the farces and pantomimes which in the past had been the fare of the vulgar and confined to such areas as Smithfield. Such activities must alarm the people of refined taste and they must apprehend the doom of culture. In the words of A.E. Williams:

> In its subject matter—the corruption of traditional literary standards, the misuse of verbal art—the Dunciad is certainty involved with the local, the personal, the contemporary.

As said earlier, the *Dunciad* is written on the epic pattern. Pat Rogers in his book *An Introduction to Pope*, writes:

> Mock-heroic is only one of a number of strands in the fabric of *The Dunciad*. Sticking to round figures, we can isolate ten elements in the imaginative design—they may be technical devices or what we generally call 'themes', but they all serve a single vision of triumphant dullness.[5]

We can summarise his explanation of the ten elements in *The Dunciad*:

1. The first element is that of mock-epic. The poem begins in the manner of the *Aeneid*. In fact, the first line of the poem is an imitation of the first line of the classical epic. This element connects *The Dunciad* to Dryden's *Mac Flecknoe, A Poem* which describes the succession of one bad poet to another. It also corresponds to the frame of *The Rape of the Lock*. But whereas, there is a sustained use of the conventions of the epic in *The Rape of the Lock*, there are occasional references to them in *The Dunciad*. Pat Rodgers concludes:

   The mockery of the epic form is there; but in *The Dunciad* Pope's primary concern is not to write mock epic but to make use of that form to satirize his enemies.[6]

2. As written in the Preface to the poem the action of the poem is the removal of "the imperial seat from the city to the polite world", just as that of the Aeneid is the removal of the empire of Troy to Latium. The poem thus is dynastic in conception. Its theme is the progress of the empire of dullness. Pope's main reason for alluding to the *Aeneid* was to set up the counter image of a heroic quest to discover a kingdom,—to found the empire of dullness in a new area.
3. "More fitful use is made of the greatest renaissance epic Milton's *Paradise Lost*. The new King Dunce is constantly presented as another Satan; Milton's figures of Sin and Death are recalled by the operations of Dullness."[7]

   Lo! thy dread Empire Chaos! is restored;
   Light dies before thy uncreating word. (IV, 653-54)

   Professor A.E. Williams argues that Pope injects a conscious devilry into his creation by stirring in our minds recollections of Milton. He writes:

   > By no other means could Pope have so readily revealed the evil implicit in duncery as he conceived it than by his parody of *Paradise Lost*, the metaphoric alliance of duncery with diabolism. Pope constructed an antitheology, an inverse paradigm of creation, where the Supreme Being is an image of nullity and destruction.[8]

4. In contrast to these traditional elements, with their memories of a noble past, we turn to a group of starkly contemporary themes. Most of them root the poem in a recent past and in a closely adjacent setting. Where the epic allusions, mainly comic, opened out the design in the first Book, these components serve to fix *The Dunciad* in a localised situation. The locale is, of course, London in the eighteenth century.

There are many remarkable similarities in the routes followed by the two processions, one of the Lord Mayor Sir George Thorold and the other of the dunces. Even the divergences appear to realize in symbolic fashion, the mayoral journey. The poet's intention is clear. The dunces represent the encroachment of City powers upon the polite quarter of the town, that is, the West End. The progress is seen less as a piece of municipal pageantry than as an arrogant assertion of the dominance of the City and the moneyed interest over the more humane values. The absurd games played by the dunces are the twisted forms of good plays by writers like Dryden, Congreve, Etherege and Wycherley.

5. Less narrowly, the poem gives us a picture of urban disorder. It images London life as a continual experience of buffeting, overcrowding, stench and squalor. Perhaps, *The Dunciad* is the first poem of a familiar modern theme—the pressures of city living. Previously, writers like Ben Jonson, Thomas Dekker and Daniel Defoe already had contrived fictions out of the city life. But Pope is more radically innovative. He seems to have the premonition of the seamy side of the city life. The uproarious goings on of the dunces is astonishingly the mode of the present-day mobs. The popular method of protest of our time was absent in Pope's days. "The point", Pat Rogers says: "is not that Pope is directly portraying the dunces as populist rioters. It is rather that he drew on his deepest fund of creative energy to build up a myth of social disorder.... He connected crowding and violence, by pure poetic logic, and thus anticipated the findings of later sociology."[9]

6. For Pope Grub Street is the most noisy rather clamorous part of the city. Most of the characters in the poem are part of the Street.... They are mentioned by name. These professional writers are characterized by their various productions. In Book I, the authors are depicted as physical objects in a mock-heroic way. Later, in the

poem, the writers take on a personal identity but they are always liable to revert to the primitive sludge that is dullness. It does not matter who is who. They are all experts in literary piracy and plagiarism. Art and poetry have no value for them. They are more interested in commercial writing.

7. The opening lines of the poem quoted earlier have the phrase "The Smithfield Muses". The place Smithfield is nearer to West End. Pope has juxtaposed the place with the place of real creation. The juxtaposition and contrast make Pope's point clear: the Smithfield writers are supplanting the serious drama. Smithfield in those days was the place where farce plays were staged.
8. There are hints of the presence of politics in *The Dunciad*. The eighteenth century writers were clearly divided into two groups: the Tories and the Whigs. As Pope himself was a Tory, he was attacked by the Whigs and in turn he, too, attacked them. In *The Dunciad* all his opponents are Whigs. This is why Theobald is the main target of Pope's satire in Book I but Cibber, the Poet Laureate, in the remaining Books.
9. *The Dunciad* is a standing rebuke to pedantry. It mimics the self-styled scholars who want to be honoured on their slender texts. It is pertinent to quote the words of Pat Rogers:

> The endless delaying tactics of the preliminaries recall Swift's *Tale of a Tub*, another anti-book which makes its own envelope a parodic weapon. Equally, the laborious footnotes impugn over-meticulous attention to verbal detail even as they slily cap Pope's innuendoes. Scriblerus is backed by the fine invention of 'Ricardus Aristarchus'. Through the persona of Aristarchus Pope makes his most direct attack on the arrogance of scholars who 'made Horace dull, and humbled Milton's strains'. The new world of Dullness is one where wits earn that name by mincing standard authors to bits.[10]

10. Finally, *The Dunciad* is a giant-sized joke. It is an extension of The Scriblerus Club gossips to the full dimension of high art. Pope has very artfully projected the ideas of his group in the poem. He has made use of the mock-epic form to satirize his adversaries. His feeling is genuine because he finds that poetasters are lowering the standard of poetry. If they had remained confined to versification only, there would have been no problem. What is painful or ludicrous is that these people, called dunces in the poem, boast of their scholarship and genius and brag garrulously of their achievements, though it is a well-known fact that their achievement is poor.

II

Only a week before the *Dunciad* was published, there appeared a letter in the *Daily Journal* stating that Pope was writing a poem to be called "The Progress of Dullness". Pope attributed the letter to his old enemy John Dennis. A.E. Williams is of the view that even if Pope accused Dennis of falsity,

> There is a possibility that this was actually the title of an earlier version of the Dunciad.[11]

The word progress is important in the title "The Progress of Dullness". The major narrative progression is the movement from "Troy" to "Latium". It is the epic metaphor of Book I.

In Book I the idea of progress from one area of London to another is sometimes obscured by the mass of satirist material with which the poem's action is burdened. The general impression is that Theobald is rapt away in the cloudy folds of his goddess-mother and set down almost immediately in her sacred dome. It seems he shall remain satisfied with his small kingdom of dullness. Pope's satire is quite pungent, when he describes the works of Theobald:

> Round him much embryo, much abortion lay,
> Much future ode, and abdicated play;
> Nonsense precipitate, like running lead,
> That slipped through cracks and zig-zags of the head;

All that on folly frenzy could beget,
Fruits of dull heat and sooterkins of wit.

(I, 121-26)

Pope's satire then moves on to Theobald's blatant plagiarism:

Next over his books his eyes began to roll,
In pleasing memory of all he stole,
How here he snipped, how there he plundered snug
And sucked all over, like an industrious bug.
Here lay poor Fletcher's half-eat scenes, and here
The frippery of crucified Moliere;
Wished he had blotted for himself before
There hapless Shakespeare, yet of Tibbald sore.

(I, 27-34)

But, there is the sign of action and movement, when he is succeeded by Cibber. This succession reminds us of Dryden's *Mac Flecknoe* where the successor is expected to do more foolish things. Here Cibber is given the throne, the sceptre and the crown:

Thou Cibber! thou, his Laurel shalt support,
Folly, my son has still a friend at court. (I, 299-300)

Now it is under the leadership of Colley Cibber the dunces march towards Westminster. A.E. Williams comments:

> In Book II the movement from one area to another is clearly delineated step by step, or rather a street-by-street fashion. The dunces go on a well-defined progress through the streets of London and begin to realize geographically the 'action' Pope claimed for his poem. From their base in the city the powers of duncery conduct an invasion of the polite world in Westminster, and the physical reality of their journey through the streets operates to supply the reader with that tangible suggestion of action, of movement and change which critics have accused the poem of lacking. In Book II, therefore, contemporary London topography is an essential, meaningful part of the poem.[12]

In fact, we are reminded throughout *The Dunciad* of the traditional celebration of the day when the new Lord Mayor assumed his office:

> It was on the day, when Thorold, rich and grave,
> Like Cimon triumphed, both on land and waves:
> (Pomps without guilt, of bloodless swords and maces,
> Glad chains, warm furs, broad banners and broad faces)
> Now night descending, the proud scene was over
> But lived in Settle's numbers, one day more.
> Now mayors and shrives all hushed and satiate lay,
> Yet eat in dreams the custard of the day. (II, 183-90)

According to A.E. Williams, this journey from the City to Westminster is symbolic of the invasion of the middle class commercial standards into the standards traditionally associated with the King and the nobility. He explains the metaphoric weight of the march of the dunces to Westminster:

> The path pursued by the dunces in their riotous peregrination about London is markedly similar to that followed by the Lord Mayor and his attendants in their journey from the city to Westminster. The pageantry of this civic event, therefore, takes on metaphoric weight. The Lord Mayor, as the highest civil authority, easily becomes, however ridiculously described, the power and affluence of the City personified. He and the City itself become, in the *Dunciad*, symbolic of certain values—and so does the court world to the West. The two areas were dedicated, however, to quite different standards of value, and when, in the *Dunciad*, the commercial and middle-class standards of the City invade the aristocratic province and corrupt the standards traditionally associated with the king and the nobility; the event is represented by Pope as a cultural catastrophe. Classical and humane letters, so long fostered by the aristocracy and bound up with humanistic ethics and ideals, appear to be threatened in the *Dunciad* by the combined onslaughts of trading-class attitudes and a debased literary practice.[13]

The correspondence between the progress of the dunces and the progress of the Lord Mayor's procession through the streets is not exact. But there are many remarkable similarities in the routes followed by the two processions. There are occasions when the dunces diverge from the official path of the Mayor.

The dunces spend a night at the sacred dome of Dullness near the Tower of London. Then the goddess and they move through the city to the site of St. Mary le Strand Church in Strand. The spot is highly significant because the jurisdiction of Westminster begins there. At this place the noisemaking contest is held. Sir Richard Blackmore is the Victor. Pope narrates Blackmore's performance in hyperbole:

> But far over all, sonorous Blackmore's strain,
> Walls, steeples, skies, bray back to him again:
> In Tot'nam fields, the brethren with amaze
> Prick all their ears up, and forget to graze;
> Long Chancery-lane retentive rolls the sound
> And courts to courts return it round and round:
> Thames wafts it thence to Rufus' roaring hall,
> And Hungerford re-echoes, bawl for bawl.
> All nail him Victor in both gifts of song
> Who sings so loudly, and who sings so long. (II, 247-56)

The word "bray" in the second line is significant. It means that Sir Richard Blackmore's voice was as hoarse and cacophonic as that of an ass. In the third line the word "brethren" refers to the donkeys grazing in the field. They prick their ears to know from where their brethren's voice was coming. Pope's satire is here really sharp and pungent.

The selection of Blackmore as the "voice" of the City powers is significant. This poetically prolific doctor is dubbed the "City Knight", the "City Bard" and the "Cheapside Poet". Being a representative of the middle class he is the most appropriate agent for the extension of city standards into the court world.

Immediately after Blackmore's fearsome song the dunces return from the Strand in Westminster to the junction of Fleet Ditch and the Thames. There, they hold the mud-diving contest.

Having completed their muddy sport the dunces proceed from the river with their goddess up the Fleet and Ludgate Hill. Then they move on through Ludgate and enter the city. The first two Books are related to journey and have a unique kind of action. Professor A.E. Williams has very succinctly commented:

> Pope's imitation of the 'action' of the *Aeneid* in Book I and the carefully identified geographical movement of Book II work together in Dunciad to suggest the conquest of a 'World' by duncery.[14]

The third Book follows the epic convention of journey to the underworld. There are two important characters: Theobald and his ghostly father Settle in the role of Anchises. When Theobald visits the under-world of Dullness as Aeneas' journeys to Hades, he is given a vision of the future glories to be attained by a race cast in his own heroic mould. It is a vision which adheres closely to one of the most widespread artistic conventions of the seventeenth and eighteenth centuries—the progress piece.

As soon as Theobald has encountered Anchises (Settle) the latter takes him to a hilltop "whose cloudy point commands/ Her (Dullness') boundless empire over seas and land". He says to Theobald:

> Far eastward cast thine eye, from whence the sun
> And orient science at a birth begun. (II, 65-66)

Together father and son then witness in a vision the dark cloud of Dullness which, rising in the east, spreads over the entire globe. This panoramic envelopment of the earth by dullness and darkness in successive stages is the portion of Book III which reflects the progress convention. Rising in China, the shadows cover Egypt, Rome, Spain, Gaul, Arabia, and finally move toward Britain. Settle says:

> And See! my son, the hour is on its way,
> That lifts our Goddess to imperial sway:
> This favourite isle, long severed from her reign,
> Dove-like, she gathers to her wings again. (III, 115-18)

Here the hidden comparison between the Holy Ghost and the Goddess of Dullness is intended for contrast. Against the traditional concept of cultural succession from Greece to Britain, Pope poses a heritage of Dullness, a progress Westward of the forces of disorder and darkness. The light of the sun is eclipsed by the forces of darkness. Settle, recounting to Theobald the nature of the coming event, exclaims:

> Proceed great days! till learning fly the shore,
> Till birch shall blush with noble blood no more,
> Till Thames see Eton's sons for every play,
> Till Westminster's whole year be holiday;
> Till Isis' elders reel, their pupil's sport;
> And Alma Mater lie dissolved in port!
> Signs following signs lead on the mighty year;
> See! the dull stars roll round and reappear. (III, 329-36)

The word "signs" in line 335 means the zodiac signs in the year. The total meaning is that the reign of Dullness is everlasting.

In the beginning only three Books of *The Dunciad* were published in 1728. It is only after writing *An Epistle to Dr Arbuthnot*, Pope decided to write the fourth Book. Pope himself considered Book IV one of his masterpieces. For A.E. Williams it epitomises the philosophic tradition long cherished by the British people. He writes:

> Into the fourth book of the *Dunciad* that was found and first published in 1742 Pope packed a whole world of traditional ethical and philosophical ideas and attitudes. Often there is distilled into a couplet the essence of an idea that had ramified for generations in the history of moral philosophy. This procedure, which introduces into the poem backgrounds quite distinct from any we have hitherto discussed, gives Book IV great richness of meaning at the same time that it creates a practically endless exegetical task.[15]

Critics like Warton, Griffin and Rogers are of the view that the progress or action of the three Books comes to a halt in Book IV. They say that the first version of 1728 was complete in itself and Book IV is an imposition and that it looks like an appendix. Before coming to examine their views it is better to see the content of this section.

In its overall structure Book IV expounds, in poetic terms, the humanist position that the segregation of words and things is fatal. Almost exactly half of the book is devoted to attempts by the dunces to exist in a merely verbal or else a merely phonetic world. First, there are the episodes of the opera. We should remember that Pope and his group objected to opera because it seemed to them to be sound without sense, and also because it appealed, in its emphasis on the spectacular to the eye rather than to the mind. Secondly, the dunces preach "the word without a call" and have the "cant of wit, without the soul". Third, there is the schoolmaster who teaches "words alone".

> Since man from beast by words is known
> Words are man's province, words we teach alone.
> (IV, 149-50)

Here, is, of course, a phrase of profoundest meaning for humanist. It is language that distinguishes man from animals. *Logos* was the term used by the Greek and the Romans. *Logos* implies speech and reason. But what the speaker here does is that he ignores the content the humanists gave to the term "words". He has emptied eloquence of its wisdom and squeezed out of the word the thought it embodies—"words alone we teach". In attempting to set words apart from thought, the speaker, a schoolmaster, violates the traditional humanist view that they are hardly separable. Pope satirises this attitude in these lines:

> A poet the first day, he dips his quill;
> And what the last? a very poet still. (IV, 163-64)

Such a poet solely devoted to words without content makes no progress and towards the end of life remains the same what he was in the beginning of his career—"a very poet still".

This practice of the dunces is not confined to school level only. Even the "Aristarch" (equivalent to the Archbishop of the English Church) of the universities declares "on words is still our whole debate". In the first half of Book IV, Pope tries to show what a misconception and misuse of the "words" leads to—debased art, "minute critics", empty-headed wits, political satraps and debauchery of private virtue.

In the latter half of Book IV, on the other hand, Pope is concerned with the perverted and irrational employment of "things". After the episode of the Grand Tour the satire revolves round the "thingful" preoccupations of coin collectors and speculators. Through the activities of such personages Pope suggests that an exclusive concern with "things" leads to irreligion and profaneness, to a despiritualized universe to a nation of irreverent dilettantes, godless naturalists, and philosophic sceptics.

A hint of irreligion appears in the first portrait following the fop's* reception. Annius, the notorious dealer in antique coinage, prays to Dullness:

> Grant, gracious Goddess! grant me still to cheat
> O may thy cloud still cover the deceit!
> Thy choicer mists on this assembly shed,
> But pour them thickest on the noble head.
>
> (IV, 355-58)

In the coin-collectors episode Pope suggests ironically that gold is the God of the nation and thus strikes at commercial values and the relatively new phenomenon of finance capitalism, which threatened traditional Christian attitude towards usury and money hoarding. He says, "Midas sits Lord Chancellor of Plays."

Immediately following the episode of the coin-collectors, the virtuosi "thick as locusts blackening all the ground" swoop in. The comparison "thick as locusts" suggests that the virtuosi have lost their human qualities in a kind of metamorphosis. The whole character of the virtuoso episode makes clear what was wrong, in the Augustan sense, with virtuosity. The tendency of the virtuoso mind, as Pope saw it, was to stop with nature itself. The florist mistakes nature's ministrations to the flower he thinks

---

* Dr. Johnson's criticism of the London fops in the poem *London* is the other example of how the eighteenth century intellectuals viewed the materialism of the middle class youth.

so highly of his own. He wrongly thinks that he has surpassed nature's power. He says, foolishly but arrogantly,

> Did nature's pencil ever blend such rays
> Such varied light in one promiscuous blaze? (IV, 411-12)

A little later the entomologist boasts:

> Rose or carnation was below my care;
> I meddle, Goddess! only in my sphere. (IV, 431-32)

An exploiter of nature, he is interested mainly in the naked fact, and that, too, when it is within his specialty.

Both virtuosi are made to appear as violators of God's Garden. As said earlier Pope accepted the eighteenth century concepts of nature and art. In *Essay on Criticism* and *An Essay on Man,* he advised poets and critics to follow nature. In other words, art should follow nature. But these virtuosi, instead of looking through nature upto Nature's God focus on nature itself and forget the Great Designer. They concentrate and specialise in "things". Their outlook is commercial. This view of life leads to the fatal insulation of human activities. They get themselves isolated from the main stream of life and lost in aberrations. Some give their exclusive attention to shells, others wander off "in a wilderness of moss" or "waken to a humming bird".

Pope emphasizes repeatedly in latter half of Book IV the idea that an exclusive concentration on the physical world leads to separation of man from spiritual values and God. The dunces are concerned with nature only. They follow the advice of Dullness to:

> .... Think their eyes
> And reason given them but to study flies!
> See nature in some partial narrow shape.
> And let the author of the whole escape:
> Learn but to trifle; or, who most observe,
> To wonder at their Maker, not to serve. (IV, 453-58)

The perversions of the dunces in the realm of nature lead inevitably to theological perversions, and so Pope introduces at this point a "gloomy clerk". The gloomy clerk, of course, is a member of the Church, but he, too, is a pervert. He is a

Sworn foe to mystery, yet divinely dark;
Whose pious hope aspires to see the day
When moral evidence shall quite decay. (IV, 460-62)

He expounds the origin of duncery in price. Dullness, he says is the goddess of pride:

All-seeing in thy mists, we want no guide,
Mother of arrogance, and source of pride. (IV, 469-70)

Earlier he preached before the dunces:

Let others creep by timid steps, and slow,
On plain experience lay foundations low
By common sense to common knowledge bred
And last, to nature's cause through nature led.
(IV, 465-68)

In this speech, the gloomy clerk's intention is crystal clear. He wants the dunces to be proud, arrogant and God-defying because other people follow nature and the Creator. What they should do is to go against the teachings of the Bible and the basics of Christianity:

Make God Man's Image, Man the final cause
Find virtue local, all relation scorn
See all in self, and but for self be born;
Of naught so certain as our reason still
Of naught so doubtful as of soul and will
Oh hide the God still more! and make us see
Such as Lucretius drew, a God like thee,
Wrapt up in Self, a God without a thought,
Regardless of our merit or default. (IV, 478-86)

Professor Williams' analysis of the gloomy clerk's long speech is worth quoting in full. I quote the significant sentences which to a large extent explain the main idea of the just quoted passage:

> The humanist view was that contemplation of the creation should lead to humility; man first had to learn his relative insignificance in the total plan so that, through a humble approach toward the creation, his rehabilitation could be

> effected within its proper limits (this is the progress of events in *An Essay on Man*). Preoccupied with *minutae*, with the part, the dunces never acquire such a perspective on man, never see the relative insignificance of their position. They are thus led to pride; their activity may lead to the 'measuring' as Pope says, of God's 'Attribute by ours', even, perhaps, to a removal of God from the universe altogether.[16]

The Dunciad ends with the speech of Dullness. The first four lines are:

> Go children of my care
> To practice now from theory repair
> All my commands are easy, short and full;
> My sons! be proud, be selfish, and be dull. (IV, 580-83)

The poem ends with the poet's perception of the effect of her speech:

> Lo! thy dread empire, chaos! is restored;
> Light dies before thy uncreating word;
> Thy hand, great Anarch! lets the curtain fall,
> And universal Darkness busies all. (IV, 653-56)

The perception of the poet is dark and dismal. We feel that in the reign of Dullness there will no moral values nor any kind of spirituality.

The Dunciad has been viewed by critics as both a low achievement and a high achievement. Ian Jack considers it quite disjointed almost a failure. He comments:

> Although *The Dunciad* contains some of Pope's finest poetry—Book IV was his own favourite work—Warton was right in diagnosing a fatal weakness: what the eighteenth century called a lack of unity and decorum: What we may recognize more readily if we call it a fundamental uncertainty about the subject of the poem, a fatal indefiniteness of purpose.[17]

Pat Rogers, on the other hand, considers *The Dunciad* a great poem and a master achievement of Pope. He quotes lines 605-18 from the poem and then gives his estimate:

> This illustrates the fact that Pope needed to be a major poet to do justice to the triumph of Dullness.... A slender talent would have been overborne by the heroic and prophetic obligations of the undertaking. Yet it was also necessary that a central comic vision should inform the poem, for one day of straight epic was done. In Pope the hour found its man, for he was learned enough not to misapply his learning, serious enough not to solemnize a farce, artistic enough not to fear stretching the confines of art.[18]

The Dunciad as I see it is a satire on those poets and critics who do not follow nature. Their art is confined to the mazes of nature. They have failed to see God whose art is nature. A true poet should see first God, then nature and then write or judge poetry accordingly. Besides, it is a satire on the rise of materialism and decline of humanism and spiritual values.

Notes

1. Ian Jack, *Augustan Satire*, p. 16.
2. Ian Ousby, ed., *Cambridge Guide to English Literature* (London: CUP, 1966), p. 346.
3. Ian Jack, *op. cit.*, p. 117.
4. A.E. Williams, *Pope's Dunciad: A Study of its Meaning* (London: OUP, 1955), p. 10.
5. Pat Rogers, *An Introduction to Pope*, pp. 104-05.
6. *Ibid.*, p. 5.
7. *Ibid.*, p. 106.
8. A.E. Williams, *op. cit.*, p. 30.
9. Pat Rogers, *op. cit.*, p. 109.
10. *Ibid.*, p. 114.
11. *Ibid.*, p. 29.
12. A.E. Williams, *op. cit.*, pp. 29-30.
13. *Ibid.*, pp. 30-31.
14. *Ibid.*, p. 40.
15. *Ibid.*, p. 104.
16. *Ibid.*, p. 129.
17. Ian Jack, *op. cit.*, p. 134.
18. Pat Rogers, *op. cit.*, p. 130.

8

Style and Technique

Every work of art has two aspects: content and form. By content, we mean the reality presented in a literary text. Form is the manner in which a text is written. According to Aristotle, content is the object imitated. The Russian Formalists maintain that it is reality embedded in the text. Aristotle considered medium, object and manner equally important. In our time, the Russian Formalists, the French structuralists and the German phenomenologist lay stress more on language and technique. The proponents of the German Rezeption—Aesthetic theory consider the reading process the formation of a good gestalt, that is, a compact and meaningful whole.

It follows then that a writer's work is not evaluated on the basis of its content or ideas alone; it is important that the ideas are presented in a good form. Form consists of style and technique. By style, we mean the author's choice of words, figures of speech and sentence structure. Technique is the method of organizing the different components into a well-structured whole. Aristotle maintained that an artistically beautiful tragedy is a whole and all its parts are whole. In addition the size of the play should follow the principle of the golden mean and the size of the parts should be proportionate to their function in the whole. It is an important task of an author to see that his or her work has "beginning", "middle" and "end".

Great writers are innovative. Confronted with the new challenges of life, they find that they cannot present them in the old way and, so, they make experiments with the existing forms. They coin new words and invent new techniques. This is why every age has its own distinct style and technique and almost all creative writers follow the general pattern of their age. The metaphysical poets are quite different from the Elizabethan poets in style and technique and so are the Augustan poets from their predecessors. It is to be noted that although all Elizabethan poets have certain common features, each important writer has his own style and technique. Scholars have pointed out the difference of style in the plays jointly written by Shakespeare and Fletcher. Pope has his own style and technique but in spite of his individuality he is a product of his age.

Pope's Style

The general characteristics of eighteenth century poetry are:

(a) Urbanity
(b) Wit
(c) Irony
(d) Humour
(e) Use of persona
(f) Use of the heroic couplet

They are all present in Pope's poetry.

Urbanity

Elizabethan poetry is largely pastoral. Wyatt, Surrey, Spenser Marlowe and Shakespeare all have their settings in nature. Waller's "Go, Lovely Rose" is typically Elizabethan. Let us take the following lines from Shakespeare's sonnet beginning with the line "Shall I compare Thee to a Summer's Day":

> Shall I compare thee to a Summer's day?
> Thou art more lovely and more temperate:
> Rough winds do shake the darling buds of May,
> And summer's lease hath all too short a date:

Shakespeare professes his love for his friend through the images from nature. In fact, the poem is set in nature and breathes in nature:

But thy eternal summer shall not fade,
Nor lose possession of that fair thou owest,
Nor shall death brag thou wanderest in his shade
When in eternal lines to time thou growest.

If we compare these lines to those of Dryden, Pope or Dr. Johnson, the contrast is obvious. Here are two lines from *Essay on Criticism*:

Envy will merit, as its shade, pursue;
But like a shadow, proves the substance true.

Whereas Shakespeare is concerned with the real object "shade", Pope leads it to something abstract. Shakespeare's background is nature but Pope's is a room in a big house with a large demesne in a town. Belinda's boating on the Thames is a fine example of urbanity in Pope's poetry:

But now secure the painted vessel glides,
The sun beams trembling on the floating tides;
While melting music steals upon the sky,
And softened sounds along the water die.

Even in early poems Pope is more interested in "garden" than in wild nature. In *The Eclogues,* Damon describes the beauty of the spring season:

Now rise, and haste to yonder woodbine bowers,
A soft retreat from sudden vernal showers;
The turf with rural dainties shall be crowned,
While opening blooms diffuse their sweets around.

Wit

Wit has been one of the important features of English poetry. Shakespeare made a masterly use of wit, especially in his comedies. The dialogues of Speed and Launce and the speeches of Feste in *Twelfth Night* are full of wit. We marvel at the wit of Feste. Puck is equally witty in *A Midsummer Night's Dream.* John Donne, added conceit to English poetry. All his secular poems especially "Aires and Angels", "Extasie", "A Valediction Forbidding Mourning" and "Death Be Not Proud" are marked by sparkling wit and brilliant conceit. In Pope's time "wit" and "poet" were almost identical. The fact is that a poet could not be called a poet unless he was a wit. Brevity and pithiness are the basic elements of wit. A witty saying must be short and pithy and in the words of Pope himself, "What was oft thought but ne'er so well expressed." It is because of his wit that Pope is the most quoted poet after Shakespeare. He speaks very wittily on wit. Wit must follow the laws of nature:

> Nature to all things fixed the limit fit,
> And wisely curbed proud man's pretending wit.

At other place in *Essay on Criticism* he comments:

> One science only will one genius fit;
> So vast is art, so narrow human wit.

First, Pope considers wit a combination of knowledge, intelligence and power of verbal communication. Wit is a gift of nature. As pride is the greatest sin and humility an indispensable virtue, nature has fixed the limit of wit. Man must remain humble in the use of his wit; pride will lead him to fall. Secondly, he must not be a jack of all trades. It is better that he confined his wit to only one branch of knowledge—"One science only will one genius fit." The main reason for this advice is that knowledge and art are quite vast and man's wit is limited.

Pope's great quality is that he is able to express great ideas in the fewest words possible. These quotations from his poetry illustrate his wit and command of English language.

1. Angels fear to tread where fools rush in.
2. What the weak head with strongest bias rules,
   Is pride, the never-failing vice of fools.
3. A little learning is a dangerous thing,
   Drink deep or taste not the Pierian spring.
4. A vile conceit in pompous words expressed,
   Is like a clown in regal purple dressed.
5. All seems infected that the infected spy,
   As all looks yellow to the jaundiced eye.
6. To err is human, to forgive divine.

It is said about the style of the famous Hindi poet Bihari that he was able to confine the vast sea in a vessel ("gagar mei sagar") and the same thing can be said about Pope's pithy style.

Irony and Humour

The main aim of the eighteenth century writers was to remove all kinds of aberration, eccentricity, pomp and show and exhort people to practise simplicity, austerity and cherish moral values. There are two ways to advise people: the first to speak of their flaws in strong words and the second to point them out with humour. The eighteenth century writers chose the second path of laughing away the follies and foibles of the society.

Satire was their main weapon to correct the erring ways of the people. However, they did not use strong words or invective in their satires. Pope's satire is mild and full of humour; irony and humour are his main weapons. In poems like *Essay on Criticism*, *An Essay of Man* and *The Rape of the Lock* his satire is mild. He is never harsh to erring poets and critics. He sets the ideals and then points out with humour their shortcomings. Here he laughs at them with an underlying irony:

> In search of wit, oft lose their common sense
> And then turn critics in their own defence.

(*Essay on Criticism*, 28-29)

A little later we come across these lines:

> Some have at first for wits, then poets passed
> Turned critics next, and proved plain fools at last.

(*Essay on Criticism*, 36-37)

In *The Rape of the Lock*, his irony and humour are at their best. Belinda and her dressing room are described in detail. What is ironical is that Belinda is herself a goddess and her priestess too. First, her dressing table.

> And now, unveiled, the toilet stands displayed,
> Each silver vase in mystic order laid.

(*The Rape of the Lock,* 12-13)

The use of the phrase "mystic order" makes us laugh mildly. Belinda is as much devoted to fashion, pomp and show as a priestess is to simplicity and austerity. The next two lines elaborate the idea:

> First robed in white, the nymph intent adores,
> With head uncovered, the cosmetic powers (13-14)

The irony reaches its height when we come across lines 25-28:

> A heavenly image in the glass appears,
> To that she bends, to that her eyes she rears;
> The inferior priestess, at her altar's side
> Trembling begins the sacred rites of pride.

The inferior priestess is Betty, Belinda's maid. The heavenly image is, of course, Belinda's. What is funny is that Belinda is both the goddess and the priestess. We laugh when we see her bending before her own reflection in the mirror. This self-admiration is really silly. The phrase "the sacred rites of pride" is certainly ironical and also foretells the fall of Belinda in the later part of the poem.

Pope's irony and humour evoke laughter and we laugh loudly when we read these lines. Lord Petre has cut a lock of her hair. She is terribly angry at the young man's audacity and insulting act:

> Then flashed the living lightning from her eyes,
> And screams of horror rent the affrighted skies.
> No louder shrieks of pitying Heaven are cast,
> When husbands or when lap-dogs breathe their last.
> (*The Rape of the Lock*, Canto III, 155-58)

Here Pope's satire is at its best. Belinda's reaction is absolutely natural. A lady of her age and stature will be certainly horrified at this kind of insult. Pope uses hyperbole to depict her horror and anger but he does not allow the scene to be tragic. Using bathos and zeugma he produces comic effect: we laugh openly when we see lap-dogs and husbands are put on the same scale; the young ladies are not more sorry for the loss of their husband than that of their lap-dogs. Pope's irony cuts to the quick and we smile at the excessive vanity of the fashionable ladies of the time. The juxtaposition of the contrasting images and employment of bathos in a masterly way is one of the salient features of Pope's style.

Pope's irony is never vitriolic; it is gentle and creates a mild ripple in *The Rape of the Lock*. But it is more truculent in *An Epistle to Dr Arbuthnot*, his autobiographical poem, where he has genuine grievances against people like Joseph Addison Cibber and Dennis who had really done damage to his poetical career. His satire becomes more pungent and sharp when he shows his tender feelings for his friend Dr. Arbuthnot and his own parents. The opening lines are typical of Pope:

> Shut, shut the door, good John: fatigued, I said;
> Tie up the knocker, say I'm sick, I'm dead.
> The Dog-star rages! nay 'tis past a doubt,
> All bedlam, or Parnassus, is let out
> Fire in each eye, and papers in each hand,
> They rave, recite, and madden round the land.

When he recounts the injustice and wrongdoings of those people whom he had helped, his satire becomes more sharp and attacking, the reason being his anguish and anger.

> Pitholeon sends to me: "You know his grace,
> I want a patron: ask him for a place
> Pitholeon libelled me—But there's a letter
> Informs you, Sir, 't was when he knew no better."

Use of Persona

The eighteenth century writers assumed the role of a social reformer. Their main aim was to correct the foibles, follies and vices of society through their creative works. The lead was taken first by John Dryden who satirized the prevailing vices. The main reason for assessing the role of a reformer was the corrupting influence of the reaction against Puritanism that began after the restoration of Charles II. After Dryden, Steele and Addison satirized the prevailing follies and a little later Pope, Swift, Goldsmith and Dr. Johnson continued the tradition. As it was not proper to be so presumptuous to ridicule people directly, the writers assumed a persona. Addison created the characters of Bickerstaff, Sir Roger de Coverley, Swift of Gulliver, the king of

Brobdingnag and the king of Honyhnhnms and Godsmith of the Chinese traveller. In the same way, Pope never spoke as Pope, the man. The only exception is his *An Epistle to Dr Arbuthnot* where he speaks in the first person:

> I never with wits or witlings passed my days
> To spread about the itch of verse and praise;
> Nor like a puppy, daggled through the town,
> To fetch and carry, sing-song up and down.

But in all other poems, his voice is impersonal and he is not Pope, the man; he is always a detached observer.

Use of Heroic Couplet

The poets of the seventeenth century certainly wrote in the standard rhythms of iambus and trochee but the lines in the poems were not always of the same length. They made experiments. Chaucer made use of rhyme royal and Spenser added an alexandrine to a stanza of eight lines. The Spenserian stanza consists of nine lines of which the last line is an iambic hexameter and the first eight are iambic pentameter. Wyatt and Surrey did not rigidly follow the Italian sonnet form. Shakespeare wrote sonnets ending in a couplet and thus deviated from the standard Italian sonnet form. Milton wrote, of course, in the Petrarchan tradition but allowed the idea of the octave run into the sestet. Both Shakespeare and Milton made use of the blank verse effectively in their poetry.

The eighteenth century poets revived the heroic couplet of the Greek and Latin classical poetry. As they wanted people to go high they spoke from an exalted platform. Nothing could be better than the heroic couplet, a two-line stanza in iambic pentameter in which both lines rhyme together. The movement of iambic metre is slow and majestic. Ballads are usually written in trochaic metre as they are associated with dance. Serious poetry is in iambic metre generally. Shakespeare used iambic metre in his tragedies. He made use of the heroic couplet when a king or a duke made a final speech.

The eighteenth century poets spoke from a high pedestal and, so, the heroic couplet suited them most. Besides, the caesura gave them scope to balance the stresses on both sides. For example, caesura falls on the third foot of the following lines:

> The skilful nymph reviews her force with care;
> Let spades be trumps! She said, and they were.

The *Iliad*, the *Odyssey*, and the *Aeneid* were written in the heroic couplet to make every action and event and noble character look grand and majestic. Pope has used it for comic effect in *The Rape of the Lock*:

> Behold, four kings in majesty revered
> With hoary whiskers and a forky beard
> And four queens, whose hands sustain a flower,
> The expressive emblem of their softer power.

This is a very apt description of the pictures on the playing cards. In the beginning, it appears that they are real kings and queens but later we come to know their real identity and laugh loudly.

The grandeur and majesty of the heroic couplet is evidently present in *Essay on Criticism* and *An Essay on Man*:

> Unerring nature, still divinely bright,
> One clear, unchanged, and universal light.

(*Essay on Criticism*)

> Observe how system into system runs
> What other planets circle other suns
> What varied being peoples every star
> May tell why Heaven has made us as we are.

(*An Essay on Man*)

Tropes

Imagery, metaphor, paradox, parallelism and juxtaposition are important features of Pope's style. In his early poetry, there is abundance of images from nature. *The Eclogues* and *The Windsor Forest* are basically nature poems. The images are fresh and vivid as they are parts of Pope's own experience:

> Now hawthorns blossom, now the daisies spring,
> Now leaves the trees, and flowers adorn the ground;

Begin, the vales shall every note rebound.

(*The Eclogues,* "Spring")

Here Orpheus sings; trees moving to the sound
Start from their roots, and form a shade around
Amphion there the loud creating lyre
Strikes, and behold a sudden Thebes aspire!

(*The Windsor Forest*)

The later poems, being urban in nature, reveal Pope's skill in the use of paradox and juxtaposition:

Words are like leaves; and where they most abound
Much fruit of sense is rarely found.

(*Essay on Criticism*)

Compression is another feature of Pope's style:

True wit is nature to advantage dressed
What oft was thought but ne'er so well expressed.

What Pope says about wit can be perfectly applied to his own style.

II

Pope's technique is that of an architect. His own house called Twickenham Garden gives us an idea of his concept of art which he called "nature methodized". He has followed the classical Greek and Latin writers faithfully. The early poems *The Eclogues* and *The Windsor Forest* are basically pastorals where Pope has followed the tradition of Theocritus, Virgil and Spenser. *The Rape of the Lock* follows Homer and Virgil and both the *Essays* Horace. *The Dunciad* follows John Dryden's *Mac Flecknoe* and Milton's *Paradise Lost.*

It seems that Pope is only an imitator of great writers in technique but, in fact, it is not so. All poets follow tradition and make innovation in form. *The Eclogues* follows Virgil's *Pastorals* but what is significant is the introduction of three characters in the first eclogue "Spring". Damon who comes first is the initiator and is followed by Daphnis and Strephon. The two shepherds vie with each other and the poem moves dialectically. Damon provides the synthesis and the poem ends with a happy note.

The second eclogue "Summer" has a new character Alexis. Here Pope has changed the narration. "Spring" is a kind of dialogue but "Summer" is a solo which is a fit form to present the sad feelings of Alexis and the decline of the season into antumn. In the third eclogue, "Autumn" there are two characters again, Hylas and Aegon. In "Spring" Daphnis and Strephon address the audience but here it is the poet who narrates their poignant feelings. Secondly, Hylas and Aegon are in contrast. Hylas is happy because he is united with his beloved but Aegon is not that lucky. This eclogue is a mixture of joy and sorrow. The final eclogue "Winter" mourns the death of Mrs. Tempest who is called Daphne. Here Pope has heavily drawn on Theocritus and Bion.

In other poems, Pope changes his technique as he is dealing with contemporary events, people and issues. He elevates iambic metre to perfection. Each stanza in *The Windsor Forest* leads to the other logically. *Essay on Criticism*, though it follows Horace largely, has its own form. Here Pope's technique is immaculate. Each couplet leads to the other. Right from the beginning of the poem his intention is to add "nature" in Dryden's theory of poetry which lays stress on "God's design". Divided into three sections, the poem is a perfect whole. The first section is the beginning, the second is the middle and the third, the end.

The first section is an advice to young poets and critics to follow nature. They can do so by studying the great poets of the past and, if they want to be good critics, they must be humble, religious, studious and free from all kinds of prejudice.

The second section which forms the middle lays stress on humility, righteousness and deep knowledge and the final section rounds up the stated ideas and counts the names of great critics who observed order, regularity and harmony in nature, especially the Earl of Roscommon.

An Essay on Man is divided into four sections, called Epistles. The Epistles are logically connected and while reading we realize easily how much pain Pope had taken in arranging them symmetrically. Patterned largely on the design of *Paradise Lost*, the poem moves from the place of man in the universe (the first Epistle) to man and his own self (the second Epistle); thence to the relationship between man and society (the third Epistle) and finally to the theme of man and happiness. Man can find happiness in being virtuous, benevolent and generous to other men. The design is perfect.

Pope's artistry is equally perfect in the mock-epic *The Rape of the Lock*. Although it is designed as an epic, it is highly dramatic. The poem follows all the conventions of the epic:

(i) invocation to a god or goddess who is a patron of poetry
(ii) use of Homeric simile
(iii) a central figure
(iv) a heroic battle
(v) a journey to the underworld
(vi) the involvement of supernatural beings.

What is of great credit to Pope is that he has made a comic effect in a serious way. There is a unique fusion of technique and style. We read and laugh but at the same are reminded of the fact that it is the small things that can make or ruin our life.

In the same manner, *An Epistle to Dr Arbuthnot* and *The Dunciad* are technically perfect poems. Pope has the ability to build these poems into a perfect whole to give us aesthetic pleasure.

The greatness of Pope's technique lies in his ability to take the best of the masters of the past—Homer, Virgil, Bion, Theocritus, Horace, Spenser, Milton and Dryden—and develop a technique of his own which is perfect and beautiful.

Suggested Reading

Works

Butt, John, ed. *The Poems of Alexander Pope: A One-Volume Edition of the Twickenham Text with Selected Annotation,* London: Methuen, 1963.

Crocker, J.W. *Works of Alexander Pope*, London: John Murray, 1971.

Elwin, Whitewell and W.J. Courthope, ed. *The Works of Alexander Pope*, 10 volumes, London: John Murray, 1871-79.

Rogers, Pat, ed. *Selected Poetry*, Oxford Classics, Oxford: OUP, 1998.

Biographies

Dr. Johnson. *The Lives of the English Poets,* Oxford: OUP, 1960.

Felicity, Rosslyn. *Alexander Pope: A Literary Life*, London: Macmillan, 1990.

Mack, Maynard. *Alexander Pope: A Life*, New Haven, New York and London: Yale Univ. Press, 1985.

Sherburn, George. *The Early Career of Alexander Pope,* Oxford: Clarendon Press, 1934.

Literary and Intellectual Background

Battestin, Martin C. *The Providence of Wit: Aspects of Form in Augustan Literature and the Arts,* Oxford: Clarendon Press, 1974.

Bateson, F.W. and N.A. Joukovsky. *Alexander Pope: A Critical Anthology*, London and Harmondsworth: Penguin, 1972.

Dobreé, Bonamy. *Early Eighteenth Century Literature,* Oxford: Clarendon Press, 1962.

Ford, Boris. *From Dryden to Johnson, Pelican Guide to English Literature*, London: Penguin, 1960.

Griffin, Dustin H. *Studies in Pope's Poetry*. Princeton: Princeton University Press, 1974.

Hammond, Brean, ed. *Pope*, New York and London: Longman, 1996.

Jack, Ian. *The Augustan Satire*. London: OUP, 1956. Criticism.

Jackson, Wallace and R. Paul Yoder, ed. *Approaches to Teaching Pope's Poetry*, New York: Modern Language Association, 1993.

Knight, G. Wilson. *Laureate of Peace*, London: Routledge and Kegan Paul, 1954.

Mack, Maynard and James Winn, ed. *Pope*: *Recent Essays by Several Hands*, Hamden, Connecticut: Archon, 1980.

Pakin, R.P. *The Poetic Workmanship of Pope,* Minneapolis: University of Minnesota Press, 1955.

Rogers, Pat. *An Introduction to Pope*, Cambridge: CUP, 1988.

——— ed. *Essays on Pope*. Cambridge: CUP, 1993.

Williams, A.E. *Pope's Dunciad: A Study of Its Meaning*, London: OUP, 1955.